MW01603004

MARKETING TO SCHOOLS:
A Textbook for the
Education Market

BOB AND LYNN STIMOLO

DEDICATION

To Carin, Leigh, and Erica who have
provided invaluable insight into the
school market.

ACKNOWLEDGEMENTS

This book would not be possible were it not for the generous assistance of a number of people. First Kathleen Bill and Tracy LaTouche deserve recognition for their diligent efforts to prepare and proof numerous versions of the manuscript and many detailed charts and graphs.

Thanks and appreciation are also due to several key school marketing professionals who generously gave of their time to render their valuable opinions regarding the content. These include Suzanne Austin, president of J. Weston Walch Publisher; Mike Baldwin, president of Market Data Retrieval; Jeanne Hayes, president of Quality Education Data; Warren Schloat, president of Sunburst Communications; and Harry Shoffner, director of advertising for Carolina Biological Supply Company.

Finally, our thanks to our clients - those of you who have given us the privilege to help fight your marketing battles. And, the rest of the staff at SMRI - those of you who did most of the fighting. This has been the arena from which the content of this book has been drawn.

Bob and Lynn Stimolo
Haddam, CT

TABLE OF CONTENTS

INTRODUCTION

This book is about school marketing. It's about how to do it and when to do it. It represents the sum of experience drawn from approximately 3,000 marketing campaigns. It is intended to give you, the reader, an edge over your competitors.

The school market industry is a fascinating one. It encompasses a wide range of companies. The largest school marketers are the basal textbook publishers. The greatest number of school marketers are the supplemental materials publishers. The next largest are the school supply companies. After that, the industry fractionalizes into many small unique segments.

Included in the family of school marketers are video and software producers, fund-raising companies, yearbook publishers, environmental awareness product producers, computer hardware manufacturers, foreign language materials distributors, physical education equipment suppliers, and many, many more. Each of these companies has some unique challenge associated with the successful marketing of their product or service. But they all have a great deal in common.

The single most common trait shared by school marketers is the difficulty in tracking the source of their orders. In other industries where direct marketing is employed, the order is received on a response device provided by the marketer. It's coded to tell from which promotion effort and mailing list the order was generated. If the order was generated by a salesman, he or she knows who made the decision, who placed the order, and what action caused them to place it. In the school market, this is not the case.

Almost all institutional sales are made by purchase order. Seldom is there a reference to a direct marketing campaign or a salesperson. Many times, the decision maker or end user of the purchase is not identified. This makes for an interesting marketing challenge.

It was precisely this difficulty in tracking sales that caused the founding of School Market Research Institute (SMRI). The Institute is first a full service direct marketing agency, second a source of information about school marketing through seminars, consulting and *School Marketing Newsletter*.

At this writing, there is no association of school marketers. The Association of American Publishers has an educational publishing segment. The National School Supply and Equipment Association is the trade association of the school supply industry. There is an Educational Paperback Publisher Association. The Software Publishers Association includes educational software producers. But there is no association for the collection, consolidation, and sharing of information about school marketing. SMRI is probably the closest to filling that gap.

The school market is really three markets in one – the institutional market, the teacher-at-home or teacher-out-of-pocket market, and the through-the-teacher market (reaching parents through teachers). We have found it to be a truly wonderful marketplace. People don't become teachers to make money. They become teachers to help youngsters.

But while the market is made up of a group of exceptional, well meaning people, it's very important to adhere to sound principles of marketing. Because the school market is also an extremely competitive one, a misstep in marketing usually has an immediate negative impact.

This book represents our attempt to help you to excel in school marketing. It's not a book of theories. It is the result of close to 40 years of combined service in the industry. Whether you're a veteran of the industry or a newcomer, we hope it will provide you with a practical viewpoint that will improve your success.

Bob and Lynn Stimolo
Haddam, CT

MARKETING TO SCHOOLS:
A Textbook for the
Education Market

CHAPTER 1

CREATING A SCHOOL MARKETING PLAN

AS SCHOOL MARKETING evolves, it becomes increasingly important that our marketing strategies be the product of solid planning. Whether working within a large conglomerate or out of your basement, a thorough marketing plan can greatly enhance one's chances for success.

Why Plan?

Those who consider themselves "doers" often have trouble understanding the value of the written plan. However, the process of planning is invaluable. It is not necessary that the plan be professionally printed with lavish graphics and beautiful binding. It is necessary that the plan be recorded along with the thought process from which it evolved including the rationale and hypothesis.

Here are four main reasons supporting the development of a written plan. First, it is necessary to look to the future. Operating "off the cuff" without any regard for the impact of today's actions on tomorrow's business is a solid prescription for disaster over the long haul. Promotion results suffer as well as the ability to provide good service to customers.

The second reason to develop a written plan is to aid in the evaluation of marketing strategies to determine whether they are worth the investment in time and money. For example, a direct mail program that needs a 10% response just to break even is most likely a very high risk investment.

The third reason supporting the written plan is that it provides a step-by-step approach to follow as well as to revise. Six months after planning, in the midst of fighting the battles of day-to-day business, it's easy to forget a critical step and jeopardize an entire planned program.

Finally, a written plan is an excellent way to provide other key members of an organization with a perspective of its goals and objectives. This is especially helpful to support personnel who may have to make operating decisions critical to the success (or failure) of a plan.

What Is A Plan?

A marketing plan is a document that states a marketing objective, provides a rationale for that objective, examines the risks and opportunities of various strategies in support of the objective, and recommends a plan of action. It may cover a single campaign, a full year, a five year period, or longer.

While there is no universal definition of a good marketing plan, the plan should address those items considered critical by the organization involved. The subjects most commonly addressed in a marketing plan are:

    I.   Executive Summary
   II.   Market Background
  III.   Objectives And Strategies
  IV.   Financial Projections
   V.   Critical Risks And Opportunities
  VI.   Recommendation (Operation Plan)
 VII.   Appendix (Related Information And Supporting Data)

Let's examine each of these components, beginning with the executive summary. Since it is, in fact, a summary, it's best if it is completed last. It should be terse, deal only with the fundamental information, and, most important, should not exceed one side of one page.

The market background is a discussion of the marketing environment. It includes the premises upon which the objectives and strategies are built. In a plan designed to market a program to elementary schools, the market background section might discuss these points:

1. The number of public, private, and Catholic elementary schools.
2. Possible different (or similar) buying habits of these institutions.
3. Availability of mailing lists.

4. Access to key buyers.
5. Timing of buying habits.
6. Environmental signs of demand - enrollment trends, funding trends, topical issues in education, etc.
7. Existing potential competitors and their estimated market share.

The points covered should be those that give a reader who is not familiar with the market the background necessary to understand the objectives and strategies that will follow. This may seem to be a simple matter, but in the school market it can be a challenge.

For example, a strategy to launch a program in the spring may not make obvious sense to one not intimately involved in school marketing. The fact that a launch is timed to take advantage of new budgets becoming available July 1, should be explained and not assumed. It is not obvious that an elementary school principal may be reached cost-effectively by telemarketing, but an elementary school classroom teacher may not. Clarifying these issues will make the plan easier to understand.

Objectives are statements defining the results desired after executing planned strategies. An example of an objective is: Attain a 20% nationwide market share in the sales of physical education equipment to elementary and secondary schools and colleges.

An example of a strategy in support of that objective is: Mail 100,000 catalogs to elementary and secondary schools and colleges offering about 20% of the most frequently purchased products at an average price of 15% below the competition to establish a quick market penetration.

Depending upon the purpose of a plan, objectives and strategies may be organized by market segment or by time. For example, a discussion of the elementary market may be separate from the secondary market. The plan may be segmented by year 1, then year 2, and so forth.

Financial Projections

The thought of preparing numerous financial projections can often be daunting. Common sense should be your guide. Review the strategies that are planned, make a reasonable approximation of return, and review the costs. If the financial section is approached in this manner, the plan should be sound and the projections should be exercises in reason.

First, review the strategies. They delineate the actions that are planned and are the starting point for investment costs. Then look at the objectives that are the key to the anticipated returns. Bring to bear the physical factors described in the market background section, and the financial projections should illustrate a valid scenario.

Figure 1 shows how a typical set of financial projections might look. All numbers should flow from specific strategies and be subjected to reasonability tests. For example, in year 1 of Figure 1 we estimate 10,000 orders from 100,000 pieces mailed along with telemarketing attempts made to a list of 10,000 prospects. The revenue assumption of 4,000 orders at $50 per order is based upon a mail response rate of 2% and telemarketing sales of 2 per hour. For some programs this is very believable, while for others it is next to impossible to achieve.

Figure 1

Three-Year Financial Projections

(All numbers in thousands)

	Year 1	Year 2	Year 3	Cumulative
Revenue				
Gross Sales	200	400	400	1,000
Gross Sales	4	8	8	20
No. Orders	10	20	20	50
Returns	190	380	380	950
Cost of Goods	57	114	114	285
Promotion Expense				
Mail Volume	100	200	200	500
Mail Cost	45	90	90	225
Telemarketing Hours	10	20	20	50
Telemarketing Cost	32	64	64	160
Total	77	154	154	385
Contribution to Overhead and Profit	56	112	112	280
Percent Return on Gross Revenue	28%	28%	28%	28%
Percent Return on Investment	42%	42%	42%	42%

In this example, all the numbers double in year 2 and remain constant in year 3. That's because the strategies assume a fall launch, and the years calculated are calendar fiscal years. In years 2 and 3 a spring promotion equal in size to the fall can be undertaken.

In Figure 1, the cost of goods is assumed to be 30%. In industries such as publishing, this assumption is realistic. In industries like school supply distribution it is far too low.

In this example, overhead is omitted. Some prefer this approach since overhead for a new program is often unknown or difficult to estimate. However, others prefer to arbitrarily assign an overhead based on a percentage of sales.

Contribution to overhead and profit is the money left from sales after subtracting promotion cost and cost of goods, but before subtracting anything else, namely overhead cost and profit. It is the net revenue minus promotion minus cost of goods. Subtract overhead costs from this *contribution to overhead and profit* to get pre-tax profits.

Percent return on investment is the profit divided by the sum of the promotion expense and the cost of goods sold. It's another measure of the endeavor and answers the question, "Of the money we actually invested in this program, what was the percentage of return we realized?" If the return is not high enough, a bank account or the stock market becomes a reasonable competitor for the investment funds.

The most important thing about developing good financial projections is that they be developed from specific sales campaigns projecting reasonable results. They should not be plucked from the air or assigned arbitrarily based on a projected market share. A 10% market share cannot be obtained simply by existing. Specific promotion plans must be in place to bring it about.

Evaluating The Plan

There are three tests that can be applied when evaluating a good marketing plan. First, is it understandable to the key members in the organization who must support it? Second, can the key assumptions upon which the plan is built be identified and are they reasonable? Third, is it easy to scan? Can readers identify those areas they want to read in detail and skip over those they don't? Submitting a plan to these three tests should greatly improve its potential for success.

CHAPTER 2

TIMING: WHEN TO MAIL YOUR PROMOTION

ALMOST EVERY SCHOOL market product is unique. Some appeal to out-of-pocket teacher purchases, some only to institutional funding. Some products are federally funded and others are not. Some are topical or "hot," some are passé and cold. Some are incredibly unique and some are intensely competitive. Each of these factors can be critical when choosing the best time to mail.

The school market is composed of two major purchasing submarkets: school purchases and teacher purchases. School purchasing includes anything paid for by school funds, from classroom materials to paper towels. Teacher purchasing includes anything paid for by the teacher, or paid for by parents where the teacher has played an instrumental role in the response (for example, fund-raisers and promotions to the parent through the teacher). Promoting these submarkets at the right time is essential to the success of any direct mail effort.

The Buying Season For School Funds

Unlike many other markets, the school market is very seasonal. Most schools operate for approximately ten months beginning about September 1, and ending in mid to late June. In addition, most school budgets roll over on July 1. Therefore, the majority of purchasing decisions are being made in the spring for the new budget that will go into effect in July with a second smaller wave of purchasing taking place again in the fall when school opens. Consequently, these are the two times during the year school marketers should consider mailing.

Figure 2 illustrates when orders are received from educators by school secretaries or when purchasing decisions are actually taking place. While the orders may be held until budget decisions are finalized, the actual decision to buy has been made.

Figure 3 shows when purchasing decisions regarding the upcoming school year are made in elementary schools. Figure 4 shows the same decision date for secondary schools.

General Rules Of Thumb

There are some general rules that should be considered regarding mail dates for the school market. While all are not always true for every school marketer, they are mostly true for many school marketers.

- **Spring mailings generate more business than fall mailings.**

Spring is the season when school expenditures are planned against new budgets which usually begin July 1. The lion's share of spending deci-

Figure 2

When Orders Are Received By
School Secretaries From Educators*

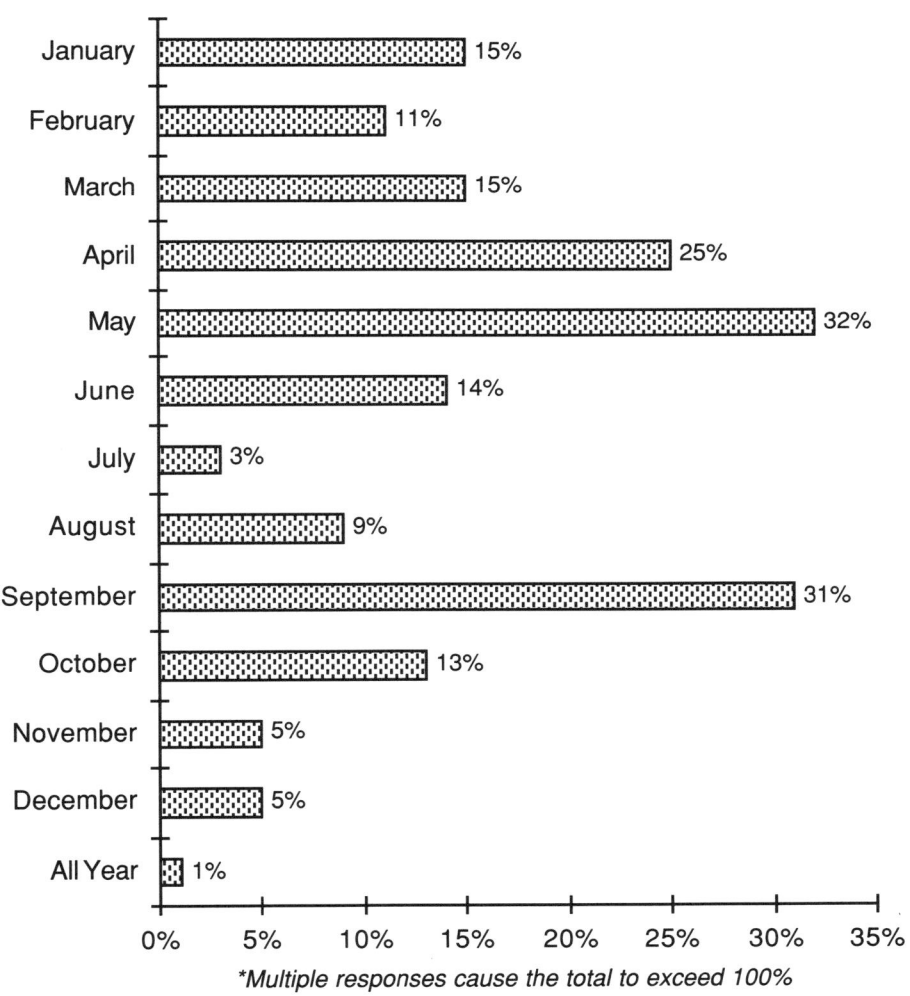

Multiple responses cause the total to exceed 100%

Source: School Market Research Institute, Inc.

Figure 3

Elementary Secretary Survey

When will your school begin to make decisions about purchases made in the upcoming school year?

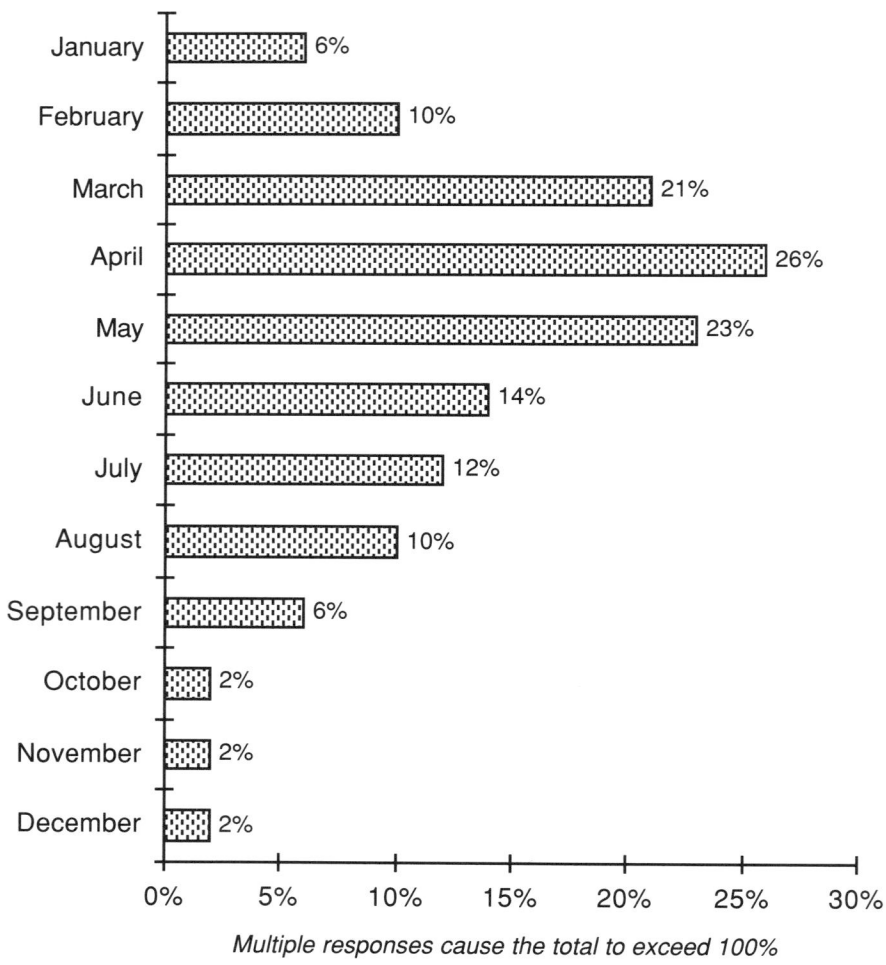

January 6%
February 10%
March 21%
April 26%
May 23%
June 14%
July 12%
August 10%
September 6%
October 2%
November 2%
December 2%

0%   5%   10%   15%   20%   25%   30%

Multiple responses cause the total to exceed 100%

Source: School Market Research Institute, Inc.

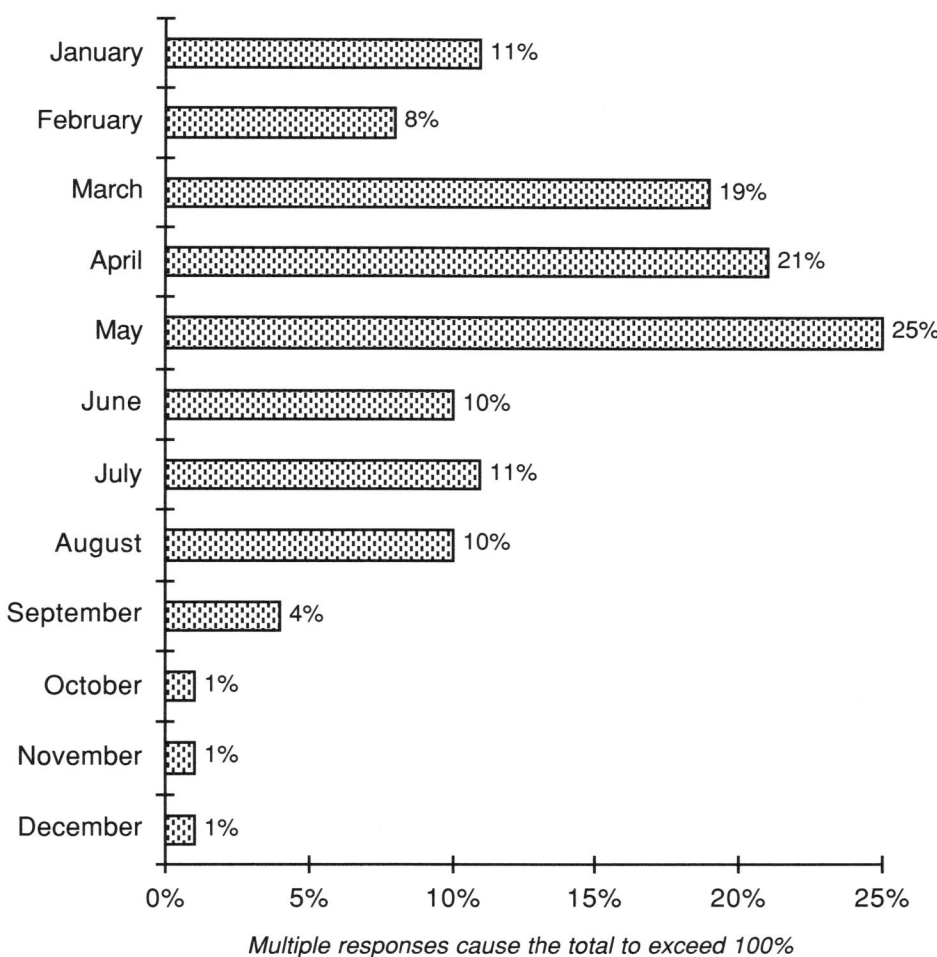

Figure 4

Secondary Secretary Survey

When will your school begin to make decisions about purchases made in the upcoming school year?

Multiple responses cause the total to exceed 100%

Source: School Market Research Institute, Inc.

sions are committed in the spring so that materials will be delivered and ready to use the following fall when school begins.

• **A spring mailing followed by a fall mailing in the same year may generate more business than the sum of a spring mailing and a fall mailing made in separate school years.**

Spring and fall mailings made in the same year will generate more business because some buyers require two sales persuasions. There are some individuals who will not order in spring but are pushed into ordering with a fall follow-up. Also, the school market is not homogeneous. While most budgets rollover in July, some of them rollover in January. Mailing in both seasons allows a marketer to pursue both types of budget rollovers.

• **It is better to use strong, competitive mailings in peak seasons, than to use any mailing in off-peak seasons.**

Simply stated, there is less money available and fewer educators making buying decisions in the off-peak seasons. Better to compete for money when it is available than when funds are scarce.

• **Multiple mailings on different drop dates can extend and magnify sales success in the spring.**

The spring season is an extended period of buying decisions. But it is impossible to know exactly who buys when. Multiple mailings over the same spring season often results in maximum sales.

• **Peak mailing months in spring are January and February for**

products that require preview and February and March for products that do not require preview.

For some products, previewing is a prerequisite prior to committing to a purchase. The preview activity takes time. If preview materials are mailed when budgets are being committed, they will arrive too late. Conversely, non-preview material mailed too early may be forgotten when the time to purchase rolls around.

Because most school bureaucracies require multiple approvals for most purchases, there is a time lag between when a teacher decides to order a product and the receipt of that order by the school marketer. When a product requires preview, as in the case of video or software, the lead time between purchase and initial promotion can be several months.

• For most school marketers, if April and May mailings deliver acceptable results, February and March could deliver better results.

For many products, April and May mailings are latecomers. Remember, many institutional purchases require several decision makers and several approvals. This takes time. April and May mailings do not leave sufficient time for many purchasing processes.

When choosing a specific mail date, several dynamics come into play including the cost of the product or service, whether or not a preview or trial is involved, the number of people involved in the purchase decision, and the type of funds that will be used in the purchase. The more time involved in the decision to purchase, the earlier the mail date.

There are five major types of buying activity in the school market. They are:

Budget Line Item: Relatively large purchase for which specific funds are provided in the budget. Includes items such as computer hardware, furniture, textbooks, seminars, and playground equipment. Usually a relatively large number of individuals can be involved in the decision to purchase. Lead time from promotion to purchase is a minimum of six months, more likely one to two years. This market requires sustained promotions throughout the school year.

Budget Category: A general spending category in the budget but specific purchase items may be unknown. Items such as supplemental materials including workbooks, paperbacks, or software, and physical education supplies would fall into this category. The number of buyers varies depending on specific items. Lead time from promotion to purchase is under six months. This market is more seasonal with promotion cycles beginning in spring from February through April and a fall cycle beginning in August.

Non-Budget School Purchases: Items required or desired by the school but not approved in the annual budget. Monies are raised through fund-raising campaigns. Items can be almost anything including team uniforms, sports equipment, awards, special equipment or supplies, and class trips. The number of buyers is often many and the fund-raising participants usually vote on what item(s) will be purchased. Lead time from promotion to purchase for most items is six months but can extend to two years. These programs are strongest in the fall. While some advance marketing can be done in the preceding spring, most is done in late August and early September.

Teacher At Home: Items purchased personally by teachers for use in school. Items include workbooks, personal supplies, classroom decorations, "how to" books, professional journals and magazines, and seminars and continuing education credits. The number of buyers is one. Lead time from promotion to purchase is a maximum of fourteen weeks. A popular time for promoting teachers at home is early summer when teachers have completed their at-school activities and are preparing for the coming school year.

Parents Reached Through Teacher: Solicitations are distributed, sent home with students, and collected by teachers. The process may or may not involve collection of money. Most programs include paperback books, posters, subscriptions, and club memberships. The number of buyers is one teacher for approximately twenty-five students. Lead time from promotion to purchase is a maximum of fourteen weeks. These programs are most successful in early fall before parents tire of multiple solicitations.

A word of caution. If mailing on a date that contradicts the logistics in Figure 2 is successful, continue to mail on that date. However, testing other mail dates to see if results can be improved would be advisable.

Spring vs Fall Buying

Is it better to mail in the spring or the fall? Will the mail pull better if it arrives before school opens or after? Will dropping the mail all at once have negative effects on campaign results? These are just a few of the questions with which school marketers struggle concerning the elusive issue of timing.

Traditionally, fall is considered the beginning of the school year. After all, this is when schools open their doors for the start of the new year. However, by fall the actual school spending year is more than half over.

As previously stated, the majority of elementary and high schools roll their budgets over on July 1. Specific expenditures for higher priced items against these budgets may begin as early as the prior year or sooner. Commitments to supplemental materials and many other lesser priced products begin in the months of March, April, and May preceding the July budget rollover.

Some research has been done to measure spring vs fall ordering activity. This research suggests spring represents more buying activity than fall. Estimates are that 60% of buying decisions are made in the spring vs 40% in the fall.

Why should this be? For one thing, there is some impetus for earlier commitment of funds. Much school purchasing is competitive. If one teacher doesn't spend available funds, another may.

Another argument in favor of spring buying is that purchasing can be done in an unhurried manner and delivery can be reasonably presumed to occur before the start of school the following year. Purchasing in the fall has the drawback that one has to wait for delivery in order to make use of the product.

A third reason why the spring season should represent a larger portion of the buying activity is that it is a considerably longer season. The spring season begins as early as January and runs as late as the close of school in June. The fall season can begin in mid-August but is essentially over by mid-October.

Using The Spring Season To Advantage

Choosing the proper mail date or dates in the spring becomes a function of overall promotion strategy and the product being promoted. Materials that do not require preview should be promoted as early as mid to late February, but generally not later than the end of March.

However, materials that are offered for preview or sold on-approval should be promoted as early as January and generally not later than the end of February. Mailing during this period should allow sufficient time for the preview to occur and an order to be placed. If mailed too late, preview or on-approval programs may not allow sufficient time to close the sale. Worse, the product may arrive after school closes in which case the respondent may forget all about the order by the following fall.

On-approval offers may also experience higher rates of return in the spring than in the fall. One possible explanation is that funding is not available until July. Therefore, the respondent returns the spring material with the intent of reordering in the fall. Three or four months later, that respondent may or may not remember to reorder.

Promotion strategy is a big factor in selecting a mail date or dates.

Some marketers prefer to spread promotion over time. Because there is a relatively sustained decision-making period for school funds in the spring, multiple hits can be made more effectively than in the fall.

A marketer faced with the prospect of a high penetration of mailing pieces per school building may be more successful dropping half the mail on two dates about two weeks apart. For example, one mailing might go out on February 15, and the second on March 1. Or sales leads may be solicited in January and February and called on in February and March. In the fall season, this same strategy could be deadly.

Because the majority of schools commit more of their full year budgets to expenditures in the spring than in the fall, it follows that the school marketer would operate more profitably by following the same logic relative to promotion budget expenditures. Therefore, promotion budgets should not be equally allocated between spring and fall. Instead, emphasis should be given to the spring.

To correspond to what is believed to be the approximate rate of purchase decisions made during the spring vs fall, a 60-40 split is recommended for most programs. That is to spend 60% of a promotion budget in the spring and the remaining 40% in pursuit of business in the fall.

This approach can be accomplished in a number of ways. First, one can simply vary the volume of mail keeping the promotion format used in both seasons consistent. For example, if 100,000 32-page catalogs are mailed annually, mail 60,000 in the spring and 40,000 in the fall.

This strategy can also be accomplished by holding the quantity constant and varying the promotion format. In the aforementioned example, one could mail 100,000 catalogs in both seasons, but the spring catalog might contain 40 pages while the fall contains only 24 pages. The variations are numerous. Depending upon the product line, promotion formats can vary among catalogs, direct mail packages, and selfmailers.

Purchasing trends also suggest that introduction of a new product be geared toward a spring release rather than a fall launch. It makes more sense to launch a new product during an entire buying season than to develop it in time for less than half a season.

One of the perpetual challenges to good timing is the Easter holiday and the traditional spring break many schools schedule to coincide near this holiday. For a number of programs this holiday can have a very detrimental effect on response. Arriving just prior to the holiday break has the effect of interrupting response. If this interruption occurs in a critical response week (usually the first two weeks of response) substantial volumes of orders may simply not be placed.

Sometimes it is better to delay mail so that it does not arrive in school the week before the Easter holiday. In other cases it may be necessary to mail earlier in order to avoid materials arriving just prior to the holiday.

How To Make The Most Of The Fall Season

There are two major views regarding fall drop dates. One view argues that education budgets, particularly for supplemental materials, are somewhat like egg timers. As time goes on, the more money is committed and the less money is available for promotions that are mailed later. This would argue for earlier drop dates ensuring that mail is present when educators return to school.

The other view argues that if mail arrives prior to or even simultaneously with school openings, it may be lost in the large volumes of mail that overwhelm educators at this time. Therefore, it is very likely to be destroyed without any reasonable consideration.

Both views have merit. However, scheduling mail to arrive in the first week of school or the week preceding is preferable. This mail should be as motivational as possible. The motivation may be a result of the package format or a powerful offer.

If, for whatever reason, it is not possible to develop a powerful promotion, then it may be necessary to let the back-to-school promotion bombardment pass and schedule the package to arrive in the second, third, or even fourth week of school. But given the options, this latter strategy is by far a second choice.

It is important to consider the product or service being sold. Products that vie against heavy competition (workbooks for example) generally need to mail earlier in the fall. Products that enjoy relatively special niches (special education products) often can succeed better with later drop dates.

Many marketers do little to distinguish fall promotion strategies from those in the spring. A product offering may be altered, the expiration date on a promotion may be changed (if there is one to begin with) and, at the most, the promotion may receive a new graphic look. However, there are a number of market factors that prevail in the fall that are not found in the spring. Many of these pose opportunities of which marketers should take advantage.

While fall is the beginning of a new teaching school year, it is the second half of the school spending year. Remember, the first half of the spending year began the preceding spring against a budget that, in most cases, turned over in July. Because it is the second half of the spending year, the fall has three unique characteristics that do not exist in the spring.

First, in the fall, purchase decisions tend to be made faster than in the spring. The budget by this time is no longer an unknown, and the start of the new year of school gives a sense of urgency to buyers. Most of the purchases tend to be made in the month of September. Therefore, the mailing season in the fall is from mid-August to mid-September so that, in most cases, promotion material will arrive at school just before, at the same time, and just after educators return.

Because response can be almost instant, school marketers have an opportunity to use a direct marketing technique that our consumer counterparts have used for years. It's known as the time-limited special offer. It is effective because it substantiates the special nature of an offer making it more credible.

A spring mailing with a 30- or 60-day expiration date can invite disaster since many educators are simply unable to respond that quickly. However, if one extends an expiration date much beyond 60 days, it can hardly be said to be motivational. In the fall, however, an expiration date between 30 and 60 days can be very effective. Despite the fact it may reduce the amount of time over which orders are received, it is likely to increase the total number of orders.

Second, availability of product is more important to the buyer. Many orders placed in the fall are for immediate use and shipping time is more of a factor when deciding from whom to buy.

Since availability is a more critical issue to buyers in the fall, many mail order companies lose sales to retailers or to the following spring season. To enthusiastic educators looking forward to employing a new product in their classroom in the fall, a four to six week shipping delay can be discouraging to say the least. If an educator needs supplies to administer a program, many might choose to deal with a local school supply company even though they might pay a higher price.

These circumstances can become an advantage by making provisions for 24- or 48-hour turnaround on one or more products and making this a key element of the promotion. One of the major elements of response is impulse. In general, the more one can capitalize on the impulse of the respondent, the more response one can expect. The promise of prompt delivery not only allays any concerns about being able to use the product quickly, it also helps buyers envision fairly immediate satisfaction regarding their impulse to buy. One note of caution: In the long run, it is important that shipping claims be fulfilled. To simply make the promise of prompt delivery but not meet it will produce more negative than positive results.

Third, because the majority of purchasing funds tend to be spent in the spring, there is generally less money available for fall buying. Estimates of the spring/fall split are 60-40 or 70-30. In other words, somewhere between 60 to 70 percent of available monies are spent in response to spring promotions and 30 to 40 percent spent in response to fall promotions.

To illustrate ordering patterns in the school market, refer to Figure 5. It shows a typical annual ordering pattern for this market.

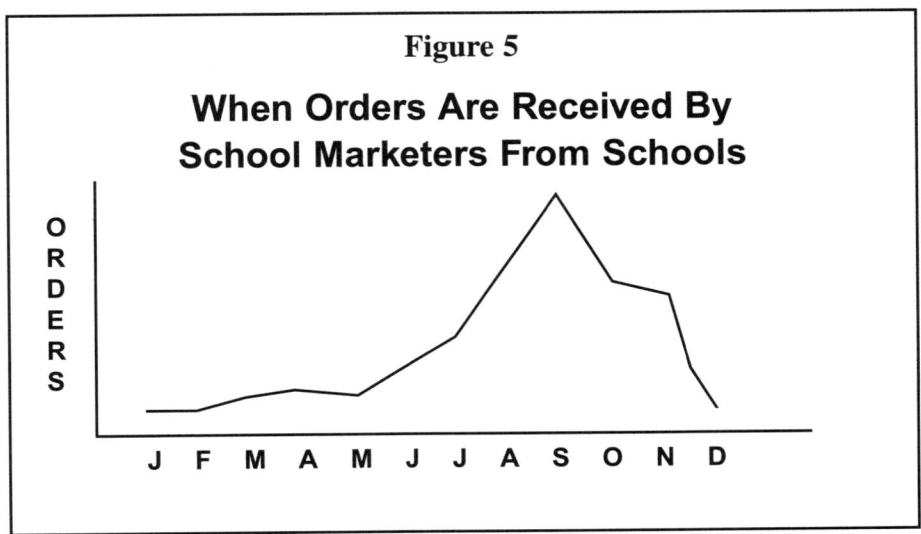

Figure 5

When Orders Are Received By School Marketers From Schools

Other Opportunities Unique To The Fall Season

There are several other opportunities available to the fall marketer, though in practice they require marketing strategies that are considerably more sophisticated. For example, the fall season is unique in its newness. It is a new school year, there are new classes, and there are new educators or older educators in new roles.

Reaching New Teachers

Two opportunities arise from this phenomenon. First, new educators and older educators in new roles can generally be more responsive than others. It is possible to select "new" educators from some education databases. An attempt to reach them can also be made through addressing techniques as well as instruction and incentives to school secretaries or through name gathering efforts.

For example, imprint a "stamp art" headline on an outer envelope or mailing piece that says "For The New Teacher In Your School." Insert several mailing pieces into a large envelope, address it to school secretaries and ask that they deliver the contents to the new teachers (or teachers in new roles) in the school. Add a small gift (such as a pen or marker) to the same package and tell the secretaries they are being thanked in advance for distributing the promotion materials.

It is possible to collect the names of these "new" educators by telephone or mail. The difficulty with this last idea is that the telephone is fairly expensive and the mail will be slow enough to hamper the ability to get promotions out to these names early in the fall season. While for certain products and services it could still make sense, a better method would be to simply rent the list from a list source.

Copy Themes

The second opportunity presented to marketers from this "new school year" phenomenon is in copy themes. Few mailings to schools are effective at reaching and appealing to this new school year psyche. The opportunity best presents itself in direct mail letter copy, but entire package themes and offers can be built around the new school year theme. The basic idea is simply to take advantage of the needs that potential buyers are likely to face at this unique period of time in the school year. A time, as we've discussed, that is quite different from that found during the spring season.

Aside from the obvious benefit of being timely and exhibiting an intimate knowledge of potential buyers' circumstances and needs, there is another advantage to topical copy themes and offers. It leads to one final point about what is unique about fall mailings.

The spring mailing season is considerably longer than in the fall, beginning as early as January and running as late as April and May. Thus, the amount of mail educators receive on any given day is significantly diluted. However, in the fall, almost every school marketer mails between mid-August and mid-September. The amount of mail an educator receives on any given day can be considerable.

To succeed in this much greater competitive environment, promotion materials must be aggressive. It is important to create the best promotion possible in the fall. Topical copy approaches and unique offers with specific expiration dates will help a promotion piece stand out in the crowd and draw response.

Teacher Purchasing

Teacher spending for classroom materials closely follows the timing and promotion cycle of that for school funded purchasing. In addition, many companies are successful mailing to teachers at home addresses in mid to late June. However, teacher participation in programs where parents are solicited, whether for premiums or school fund-raising activities, is a completely different timing cycle.

The most successful mail dates for parent-solicited programs tend to be early in the school year before teachers have reached their limit of participation in programs of this nature. However some programs (especially those that promote a "summer" theme) have success in the spring. The most popular mail dates are early September, late December or early January, and March.

The September date brings mail to teachers and students fresh at the start of the new year. Aside from being a good atmosphere for parent programs, it's a good mail date for fund-raisers as well. Many schools have unique fund-raising activities taking place at different times. The September mail date allows a fund-raiser to consider a program before plans are made for the year.

"Bad" Mail Dates

As one can see, timing is a critical factor in the marketing of school products and services. In the case of the institutional purchase, the bureaucracy buys strictly on its own schedule. November, December, June, and July are months in which to avoid mailing when soliciting most school-funded business. By November, most of the school spending is committed and a promotion of any considerable size is almost certain not to provide the necessary return. By June, most schools are preparing to close and are preoccupied with that activity. Decision making for the spring is either over or close to it. In June, many schools are already closed and by July, only year-round schools are still open.

While products purchased by individual teachers offer a more flexible mailing schedule, the demands of the school year activities preclude certain mailing times. Let's look at a couple of typical scenarios.

A fall mailing has run behind schedule. October 1, is the earliest the mailing will drop. Some marketers believe that this is not a problem because the mail will be received when there's no competition. This situation could even result in a better response. Odds are that the campaign about to be launched will have disappointing results.

Why? Because if it is an institutional sale, the promotion will arrive when most budgets are expended. If it is a teacher out-of-pocket sale, the buyer is too busy meeting the demands of his or her profession at this time. For the majority of school marketers, November and December are the worst months of the year in which to mail.

Many companies have a limited promotion budget so they make one mailing per year. Perhaps their mail drops just after Labor Day, giving teachers a chance to settle down. An acceptable response rate is received so everyone is comfortable with the mailing pattern. However, is the best return being realized on the promotion investment? Probably not.

There is considerable evidence that a significantly larger number of purchases result from spring mailings than from fall mailings, especially if they are institutionally funded. School budgets are 100 percent open to expenditure commitments in the spring. However, by the time September rolls around, anywhere from 60 to 80 percent of the budget may be committed. A fall mailing is competing for a relatively small piece of the institutional spending pie, whereas a spring mailing has a shot at the total budget.

Exceptions To The Rules

As always, there are exceptions to the rules. Three notable ones are school library marketers, school supply companies, and fund-raisers.

In many cases, the school library market is not as volatile nor as seasonal as the education market. A possible explanation for this is that the library budget is often separate and distinct and administered autonomously by one person. Therefore, it is spent in a more controlled manner and with more company and brand loyalty. While most spring and fall mail dates work as well for school librarians as for educators, many library marketers seem to be successful mailing considerably later in the fall, even as late as early November. Conversely, many library marketers are able to mail as early as January 1, in the spring.

Many school supply companies also favor January release dates. Often the promotion materials mailed are very large catalogs of 500 or more pages. These materials resemble reference materials held and used over long periods of time more than mail order materials that generate orders over a few short months.

As previously mentioned, fund-raisers are not able to follow the fall to spring scenario outlined here. While many points made about the fall certainly apply to fund-raisers, very few advance fall orders are placed as a result of spring mailings. The fund-raising industry does have a spring season, but it begins with January 1, mailings. By Easter, the fund-raising season is about over.

Deciding The Undecidable

Timing is a complicated issue. It is next to impossible to test and measure the effectiveness of various drop dates. Even if this was possible, school opening and closing dates and many holiday breaks shift every year.

Keep in mind that there are two aspects of timing that are critical to successful school marketing. First, if at all possible, an organization must maintain a presence in the marketplace in both the spring and the fall. Too many schools differ in their buying habits. Mailing only once a year is insufficient to accommodate the majority of the marketplace.

Second, mail dates must be consistent. In the Ten Commandments of Direct Response Marketing, number one is ***Thou shalt never miss a*** *mail date*. Missing a mail date can destroy the profitability of a promotion, particularly if it was traditionally mailed at the same time each year.

If mail dropped September 2, and March 15, last year, it should mail on the same dates the next year. An organization should be disciplined to regard mail dates as sacrosanct. As a customer base is developed and goodwill established, customers will come to expect mailings at the same time each year. Unless clear evidence has been established that a change in drop dates will improve business, shifting dates runs the risk of losing loyal customers.

CHAPTER 3

APPEALING TO EDUCATORS

CREATING SUCCESSFUL PROMOTIONS for any market is not an easy task. Identifying a market's unique characteristics can be a key factor. When addressing educators, it is important to remember what makes them unique as well as what they have in common with other groups.

Teachers Are Important

Teachers are important to school marketers because they represent access to three large yet distinct markets. They influence institutional spending; they influence parents spending in support of their young-sters' education; and they spend their own personal funds in support of their professional activities.

Teachers are, perhaps, more important now than ever before. The days when all one had to do was to demonstrate the educational validity of a product to succeed are long past. Today's educational market is fiercely competitive by comparison. Whatever the product or service, if teachers are involved in its purchase or use, it is critical to understand how to appeal to them.

Key Elements of Appeal

There are three key elements that appeal to teachers. They like products and services that are attractive, practical, and cost justifiable.

Appearance

Products that are "attractive" have several effects on teachers. They make them feel competent or "with it"; they make them feel "young" (professionally speaking of course); and, perhaps more important, they impress others including students, colleagues, and administrators. Products that are new, interesting, or flashy have the best appeal.

To maximize product appeal, employ good product management. If a product is suspected to be suffering from old age, drag it out of the closet for the "new and improved" treatment. This may include changing the name or adding a subtitle as well as adding new features. If the product isn't inherently attractive, modify it to improve its appearance. As an example, even the most drab product can be "dressed up" with a colorful classroom poster.

In addition to making items attractive through product management, make them appealing through advertising. Show products being used by attractive, eager, contemporary people. A classroom scene that's truly exciting can create as much if not more interest in a product than a headline or letter.

Practicality

In addition to being attractive, a product or service must also be practical. The most important thing to remember is that a product must help teach what **must** be taught, not what **should** be taught.

It would be wonderful if empathy and generosity toward one another could be taught to our young people. Certainly it's something that **should** be taught to children. But it's not a subject mandated by most states' department of education. And many teachers, while they may think it's a wonderful idea, will be hard pressed to draw a relationship between their jobs and programs of this type.

Consider another example. Educators don't want products that yield **perfect** math scores. What one has to do to implement such a program and achieve that result probably isn't worth the time, trouble, or money. As a practical goal, teachers look to **improve** math scores.

Most teachers submit teaching plans that show the curriculum they will present for a semester. For the most part, these plans are consistent with state department of education guidelines. The more a product or service helps teachers to meet their teaching plans, the more practical it is perceived. Products that don't address curriculum needs are often considered frivolous and impractical.

There are other important measures of "practicality." For example, a product or service must be relatively easy to use. Few curriculum software products near the sales levels that printed materials attain. That's because a great many more teachers find it easier to use printed materials than they do computers due to either availability or knowledge of necessary equipment.

Another set of problems can arise when a product is actually practical and easy to use, but very difficult to explain. For example, a company has a manipulative device that makes it much easier for youngsters to learn their math tables. This company conducted a variety of studies that resulted in a very compelling case for the merits of the product. However, it was extremely difficult to explain exactly how to use this product in a direct mail promotion. To encourage educators to "see for themselves" the effectiveness of the product, product samples were included in the promotion package. Although the mailing was more expensive, it yielded successful results.

To be practical, a product must also exhibit some demonstrable results. Educators must somehow be able to see a tangible benefit to a product or service. It doesn't have to be earth shattering. However, it does have to be enough of a benefit for the teacher to conclude that the time and money invested in its purchase and use was worthwhile.

Cost Justifiable

Whether paid for by institutional funds or out of a teacher's pocket, a successful product or service should be cost justifiable. But don't leave the justification argument to potential purchasers for they may fail to make as strong a case as you, the marketer, can present.

As the cost of the product or service rises, the need for a strong cost justification argument increases. Along with the increase in price comes an increase in the number of individuals necessary to agree on and approve the expenditure. In some cases, cost justification is the **sole** reason for deciding whether or not to purchase.

Some products and services lend themselves to cost justification better than others. It's relatively easy to cost justify an educational consultant who promises to deliver more state and federal funding through a change in a school's organization. It's a little more challenging to cost justify a general promise of improved curriculum scores.

Converting price into cost per end user such as dollars per teacher or pennies per student can help the cost justification argument. But sometimes cost justification takes more emotion than math. For example, "If just one child is spared the trauma of child abuse, this program will have been well worth over 100 times its cost!" Finding the best way to cost justify a particular product or service is a unique creative challenge.

Educators are a mixed bag. No one creative approach works for all. In fact, it's best to use several different approaches and create a media mix to maximize appeal. Remember, it's a cold and competitive world. The fact that a product or service exists is simply not enough to motivate a purchase in today's market.

Educators Are People Too

One of the most common misconceptions regarding teachers is that they are somehow superior to average people. Their academic backgrounds serve to make them immune to those marketing techniques that turn the rest of us mere mortals to jelly. Not true! Despite what educators may lead marketers to believe at trade shows or focus sessions, they respond to the same types of buying incentives that motivate the rest of the world. Free gifts and substantial discounts are as attractive to an educator as to anyone. In fact, some educators have come to expect such motivators as free freight, educational and quantity discounts, money-back guarantees, and free gifts with every order and they won't respond to promotions that lack these elements.

Keep Your Copy Clear

Just because copy is directed at educators doesn't mean it must contain complex words or sentences. Educators are deluged with an overabundance of direct mail and, like all of us, are pressed for time. Their decision whether or not to investigate a promotion takes virtually seconds. As with any other group of recipients, the promotion message must be quickly and easily understood.

Use short sentences and simple language. Heads, subheads, bullet statements, and/or graphics can enhance copy by making it easy to scan. These elements enable readers to choose the items in which they are most interested and easily identify them for closer inspection. Unless it's necessary to describe a uniquely complex piece of scientific equipment, for example, stay away from technical terms only an expert is able to understand.

Product Benefits May Surprise You

Stating product benefits in almost any promotion is highly recommended. However, many educational marketers believe that benefits should be described in terms of what a product can do to help students. In fact, educators are usually more interested in benefits that apply more directly to them.

A math program that can make students learn multiplication faster is a benefit. However, that benefit should be stated in a way that is most appealing to the educator. For example, state that the math program leaves more time for the teacher to devote to other important matters. The teacher is much more able to personally identify with the benefit stated in those terms. There are other benefits educators can appreciate. Here are a few examples:

• Teachers' guides make teachers' jobs easier by reducing lesson planning, by including test questions and answers, and/or containing everything a teacher needs to present the material easily and effectively.

• Discounts are always motivational. While they may be stated either in terms of a percentage or dollars saved, always express a discount in the most appealing manner. If the absolute dollar amount of the discount is small, mention percentages, or vice versa.

• Workbooks and/or drill sheets can reinforce lessons easily, provide a measure of student progress, and eliminate the need to prepare test materials.

Make Ordering Easy

Remember, the education market is a massive bureaucracy. Purchases must sometimes be approved by several layers of management.

Purchasing procedures vary with every district and sometimes among buildings within districts.

Offering various methods of payment such as check with order, "bill me," and purchase order options is recommended. Accept credit cards if possible. Ask for a "Bill To" address if it is different from the "Ship To" address. To reduce the risk of fraudulent orders, state that the product can only be shipped to a school address or ask for a phone number to confirm orders. Toll free telephone and fax numbers are advisable. This gives the educator the option of ordering quickly and easily without personal expense or additional cost to the school.

Keep Risk To Buyer Low

Educators may be held responsible for their purchases by their superiors. If a product does not fit their expectations or needs, they want to be able to return it easily for a credit or refund. They may wish to preview or accept product for a trial period at no obligation. Good customer service and quick replacement of damaged merchandise are also desirable features.

Librarians Offer Unique Opportunities

There is no such thing as a typical librarian. The matronly, quiet, and reserved stereotypical librarian that may have existed a decade ago certainly doesn't exist anymore. To succeed in the school and public library markets, one has to understand the modern library. Librarians range from professionals educated in this field to part-timers and volunteers. Some manage vast empires of public main and branch libraries. Others service so small a school or community as to rely on other libraries as a source of new materials.

Large public or college libraries are likely to contain a healthy dose of educated professionals schooled in the latest cataloging technologies and cognizant of the importance of fiscal responsibility and circulation management. The highest concentration of specialists such as juvenile and reference specialists, as well as many others will also be found.

Large elementary, junior, or senior high school libraries will also contain professionals, though they may be forced to be less specifically involved than their public and college library counterparts. Only very large or very wealthy el-hi schools can afford to staff numerous specialists. Smaller public libraries, whether branch or main, and smaller school libraries are more likely to employ para-professionals. Although this may be a function of low budgets, it is often a function of a lack of available professional staff from which to draw.

However, librarians with and without formal degrees in library science have available today more education programs and information sources and services than at any other time in history. Partly as a result, librarians are more business oriented and act more professionally than ever before.

A librarian's responsibilities include managing a budget, selecting new materials, securing existing materials, keeping track of circulation, and promoting and improving circulation and other library services. An attractive product or service is one that accomplishes any one of these tasks and can be cost justified. When it comes to identifying products or services that are meaningful to librarians, marketers who understand their audience and who focus on those areas that help librarians accomplish their jobs are more likely to be effective.

Choosing Media

Educators are as responsive as any business-to-business market relative to media choices. The best approach to selecting media is to begin with what seems suitable for the proper explanation of the product and offer. Then, as one gains experience with different media choices, evaluate the cost per order and settle on those media that yield an acceptable range of results.

Over the years, educators have often been denied the more creative aspects of direct mail and other media efforts because of the strong perception among marketers that such promotion would be offensive or ineffective in this market. Experience shows that this premise is not true. Educators are as interested in an unusual piece of mail as anyone. It may have even more impact in the education market simply because there is a large amount of mail and so much of it is so conservative.

Unusual mail includes the full gambit from four-color unique art, large show-through windows and polybags to die-cuts, tokens, and enclosed samples. The possibilities are limited only by one's imagination. In and of themselves, these devices do not guarantee a successful mailing. But combined with a good product or service and a good offer, they can more than pay for their expense and effort.

Educators can also be receptive to both space advertising and telemarketing. Space advertising, for reasons that are not clear, seems more effective in periodicals for librarians than, say, periodicals for classroom teachers. Not in terms of inquiries or free sample requests, but in terms of net paid orders.

At certain times of the year, most notably early fall, telemarketing can be effective as well. When telemarketing is employed, the same rules for good telemarketing apply to educators as to any other group of individuals.

Making An Offer

Having had the opportunity to explore a host of offers (free 30-day trial examinations, special discounts, and premiums) experience shows that all variations can succeed. It isn't that one type of offer is better than another so much as one type suits a particular product or service better and gives the whole presentation clarity and impact. When it comes to creating a good offer, the question is not, "Do educators respond to premium offers?" The question is, "How can educators be encouraged to invest their time to evaluate a product or service, and can a compelling case be made for a product or service in a short time?"

One of the great mistakes of which many marketers are guilty is **presuming** readership. Because educational materials are being sold, it is presumed that most educators will make the time to wade through promotion literature. The fact is that most educators will not take the time. Those who might become interested through a compelling sales presentation simply won't make the time to read a non motivating promotion.

Developing A Creative Approach

It's the responsibility of copywriters and designers to **seduce** readership. This job can be made easier through a compelling offer such as an impressive discount, free gift, or 30-day free trial examination. But with or without these tools, copy and design must still be inviting, interesting, and intriguing.

To better understand how to appeal to the education market, it helps to know something about the day-to-day existence of an educator. For example, consider a sympathetic approach to invite readership by using empathy in headlines and key phrases. Or take a straight-forward cost justification approach. Whether employing empathy or cost justification, a good design that integrates the verbal as well as visual message is as important in the education market as it is in any other market.

There are few promotion techniques that cannot be used with educators. Highbrow image design doesn't have a corner on the market. In fact, humorous and unusual creative approaches are still rare enough as to command a disproportionate amount of attention and readership. In today's market, it takes a fresh promotion approach to overcome the increased competition.

CHAPTER 4

WHAT MAKES A PROMOTION STAND OUT?

EDUCATORS RECEIVE LARGE volumes of mail, all of which compete for their attention. One of the most challenging objectives faced by direct response marketers is making a promotion stand out from the rest of the mail. There are only a few brief seconds in which to convince readers that they should further investigate what is offered in any promotion. Consequently, methods have been devised to enhance the attractiveness and interest of mailed promotions. Some of these techniques include special offers, clever designs, enclosing a product sample, or simply relying on the fact that the product is the best (or only one) in the marketplace.

Great debates have taken place over which method is more effective and how to achieve the best results. Of course, type of product, promotion format, list selection, and timing all play a role in a promotion's success. However, the bottom line of almost every direct mail campaign is cost per order. The results that must be achieved in order to justify the promotion cost should be determined in the beginning of the promotion planning process. A realistic answer provides a framework in which to plan a mailing.

School Secretaries Speak Out

School Market Research Institute, Inc. conducted a survey of school secretaries regarding the buying habits of educators. The results of one of the questions included in that survey sheds some light on what can contribute positively to the initial impact of a direct mail promotion.

The survey asked, "What element(s) of a direct mail promotion attracts your attention?" The school secretaries surveyed were asked to choose from among design, offer, sample enclosed, product, or other. Figure 6 illustrates the responses.

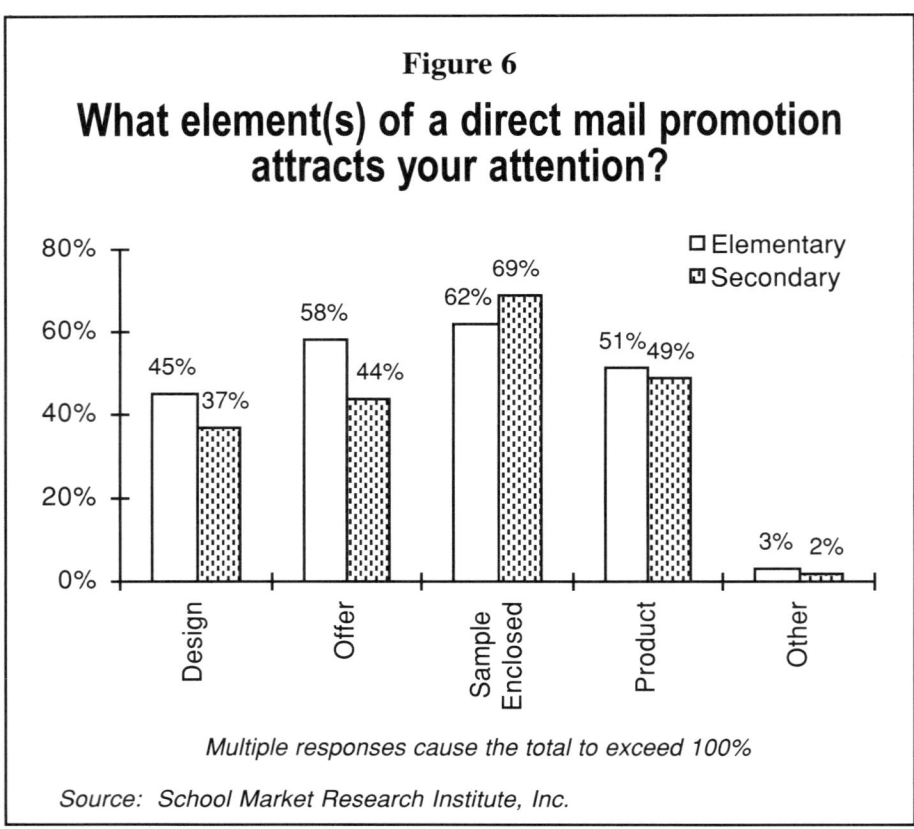

Figure 6

What element(s) of a direct mail promotion attracts your attention?

Multiple responses cause the total to exceed 100%

Source: School Market Research Institute, Inc.

As you can see, results from both elementary and secondary school secretaries were strikingly similar. Sample enclosed was ranked as the most effective attention-generating technique followed closely by offer and product. Design was also indicated as having a significant effect on the recipient's level of interest in the mailing. "Other" responses included promptness of delivery, environmental consciousness, and the comment that "gimmicks" made no difference.

Survey participants were also asked to rank those elements of a promotion that most attracted their attention. Figures 7, 8, and 9 illustrate their responses.

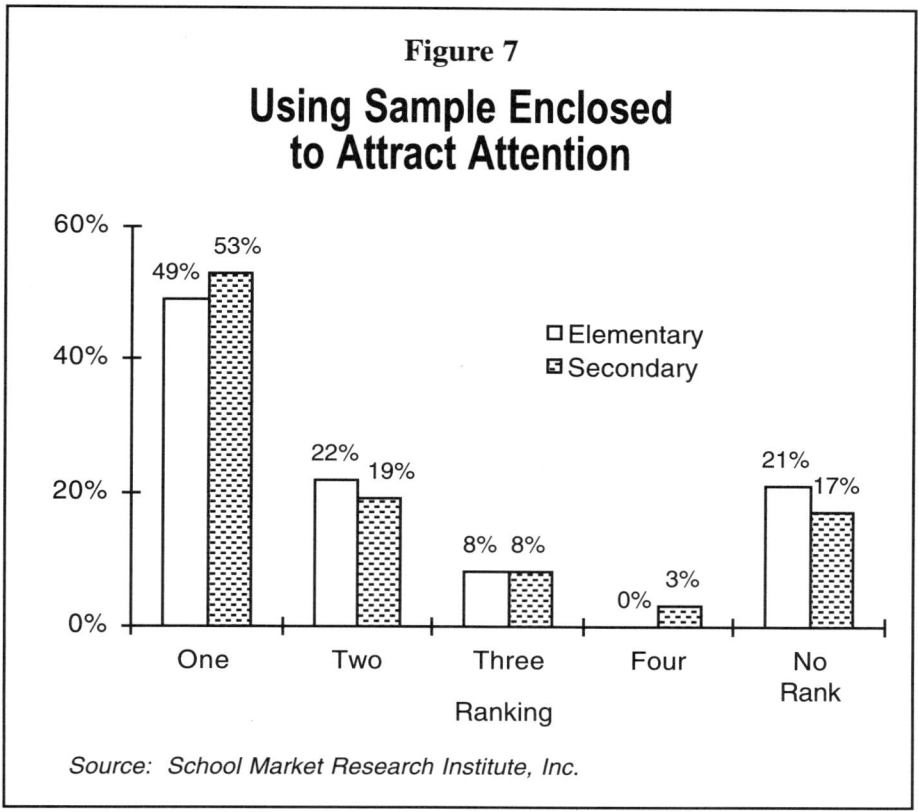

Figure 7

Using Sample Enclosed to Attract Attention

Source: School Market Research Institute, Inc.

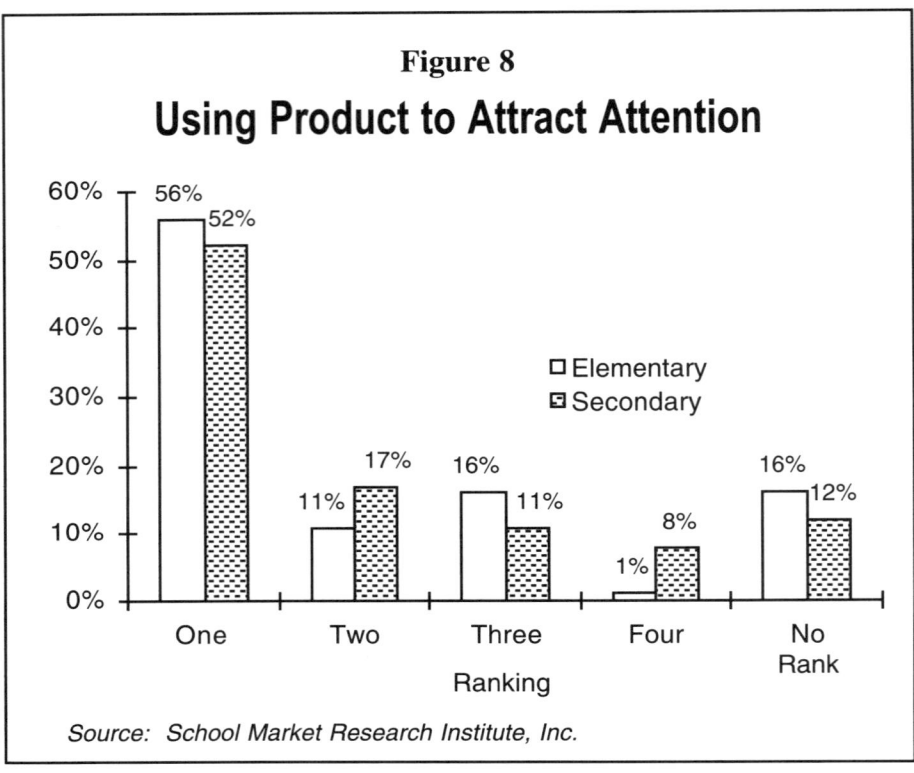

Figure 8

Using Product to Attract Attention

Source: *School Market Research Institute, Inc.*

Sample enclosed and product were indicated as the most significant methods of achieving promotion recognition. Of the 62% of the elementary secretaries who indicated a sample enclosed attracted their attention, 49% ranked it as number 1 in importance. Of the 69% of the secondary secretaries who responded, 53% ranked sample enclosed number 1. Of the 51% (elementary) and 49% (secondary) who indicated product attracted their attention, 56% (elementary) and 52% (secondary) ranked it as number 1. Offer lagged slightly farther behind as the majority (39%) of the 58% of elementary secretaries who chose this category ranked it number 2 in importance. 34% of the secondary secretaries ranked product as number 1 while 28% ranked product number 2.

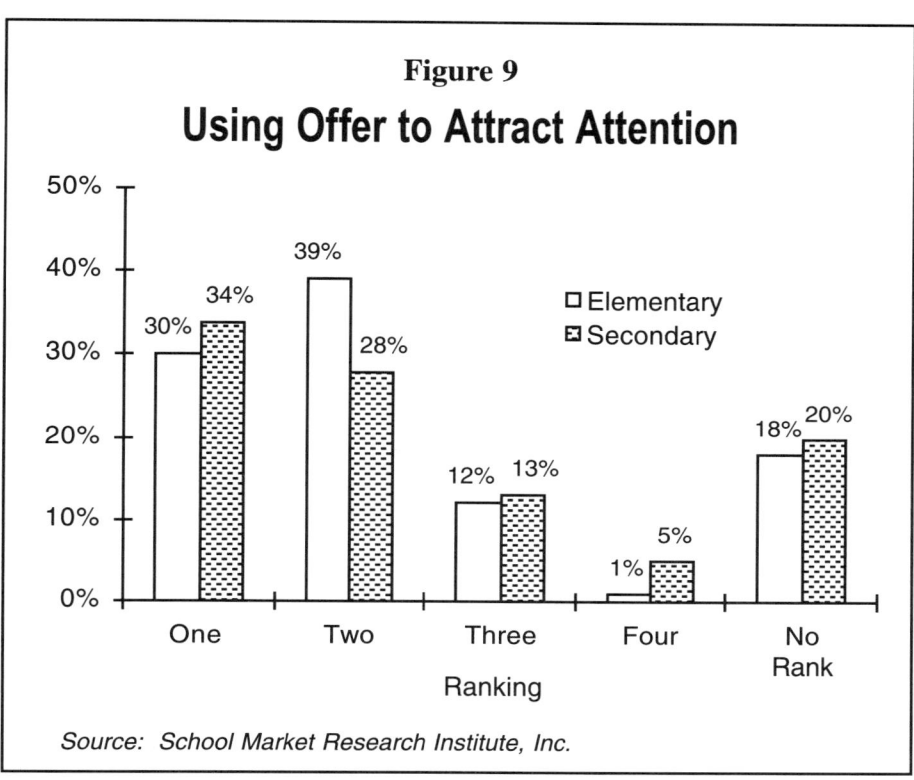

Figure 9

Using Offer to Attract Attention

Source: *School Market Research Institute, Inc.*

Mailing Product Sample

Certain conclusions may be drawn from this data. If it is possible to enclose a sample of a product in a promotion, it may pay to do so. Obviously a promotion format should be chosen that lends itself to this technique. For example, enclosing a 16-page workbook can be easily accomplished if the format is a 9" x 12" direct mail package, but is not feasible if mailing a self-mailer. As an alternative, a self-mailer could illustrate sample pages from the workbook to give the reader a sense of its contents. However, this technique does not match the attention-getting power within the first few seconds of contact with a prospect that a complete sample will have.

Since the first objective of enclosing a product sample is to draw attention to the promotion, the fact that a sample of the product is enclosed should be prominently displayed on the outer envelope. Clear polybags should be considered if the appearance of the enclosed product would add interest by showing through the outer envelope. For example, a package containing a magazine that includes an attractive 4-color cover would benefit from this treatment.

Lumps and Bumps

Not all products lend themselves to being easily mailed as samples. For example, when marketing audio-visual equipment, it's not practical nor economical to enclose an overhead projector. However, a CD-ROM containing a sample of a program could be mailed more easily. Or consider a part of a product for use as a mailed sample. For example, a direct mail package promoting audio visual materials was mailed to dealers. The product sample enclosed was the cushioning for an ear piece from a headset. The quality, design, and comfort of the ear piece was a selling point so it not only added an interesting, envelope-opening lump, but provided a theme for the mailing.

Lumps and bumps enclosed in a direct mail package almost always ensure that the package will attract attention. Pens and pencils are perfect for this approach. Even if they do not relate to the product being promoted, they will probably get the package opened and could be imprinted with a company name, address, and toll free number to help speed a written or phoned response.

Another interesting though perhaps painful conclusion that can be drawn from the results of the secretary survey relates to product. If the recipient of a promotion is not interested in what is being offered, there's not much that can be done. Of course, this argues for competent list selection which is a large contributor to every successful direct mail campaign. However, although the market may have been perfectly targeted, if that math teacher does not have the need or funds for new textbooks, the chances of having the promotion opened are greatly reduced.

Making An Offer

The secretary survey results also argue for marketing quality products, using guarantees of customer satisfaction, and providing efficient and competent service. What does all this have to do with getting a promotion noticed? Any or all of these benefits can be used as "teasers" or motivational copy that will help make the mailing stand out. For example, copy such as "All products have a lifetime guarantee" or "All orders shipped within 24 hours" indicate impressive benefits that can generate reader interest and encourage further review of the promotion.

The survey also indicates that the offer plays a significant role in attracting readership. Discounts, free product or gifts, previews, and 30-day trials with no obligation to purchase are all strategies that can be used to create a motivational offer. Keep in mind that the higher the stakes, the more attention that can be generated.

For example, savings of less than 10% is probably not worth mentioning unless it translates into significant dollars ($10 or more). In this case the savings should be expressed not as a percentage of savings but as a dollar amount. On the other hand, there is a fine line between a motivational offer and one that can have a detrimental effect on response. Savings of more than 50% may seem unrealistic and the credibility of the offer and product may be challenged resulting in decreased readership.

Attractive design should also be incorporated. Good direct mail design makes scanning easy, prominently lists benefits, illustrates the product as precisely as possible, and focuses on offers that motivate. But remember, the goal is not to create a work of art. The object is to get the reader interested in the product in 12 seconds or less.

These survey results can serve as a guide when planning a direct marketing campaign. If circumstances allow, consider some form of product sampling. If product sampling doesn't fit the circumstances, then beef up the offer and communicate product benefits to their fullest. Keep in mind that quality products are a must for any hope of continued marketing success.

CHAPTER 5

DEVELOPING SUCCESSFUL PROMOTIONS

THE GREAT MAJORITY of school marketers do not conduct direct mail tests. Most are simply unable to do so because they do not have the fiscal resources to develop systems for overcoming the "purchase order phenomena." That is the term used to describe the fact that order devices are seldom received from customers, making tracking response all but impossible.

How is one to make profit and sales progress under these conditions? The fact is that many school marketers exist at the mercy of the marketplace. Promotion after promotion is generated that incorporates strategies based on rationale rather than actual results. These efforts generally avoid major change or the incurrence of great risk.

Being specialists in school marketing offers the relatively unique position of having participated in promotion efforts for numerous clients. As a result, we have seen various response improvement attempts applied by a wide spectrum of companies serving the school market. Some efforts have been successful while others have not. Following is a discussion of the basic elements that contribute to response along with some suggestions for improving return.

List Selection: The Single Most Important Element Of Response

Most everyone agrees how important targeted lists are to proper list selection. At the same time, few marketers actually put this idea into practice. Here are some general guidelines for selecting lists:

1. Smaller mailings to more productive segments often produce greater profitability than larger mailings.

2. Schools in urban areas tend to be considerably less productive to many direct mail programs than schools in rural or suburban areas.

3. Schools with lower per pupil expenditures often buy considerably less than schools with medium or high per pupil expenditures.

4. Smaller schools often buy less than larger schools.

Obviously, one can only make use of these suggestions using data base lists. However, these lists are usually far superior to directory compiled lists.

Clearly, data base lists are more expensive than directory compiled lists. However, experience shows they are well worth the additional investment. Remember, on average the list is less than 10% of the mailing investment, but it contributes to at least 50% of the response. With that kind of relationship, it is well worth the investment of a few more dollars per thousand.

Here are some additional considerations with respect to list selections:

5. It is possible to mail too many educators in one building. Mailing all of the teachers in a school building can be the quickest way to develop profit problems.

6. For some products, the most productive individuals to which to mail are elementary school principals (by name) and secondary school department chairpersons (by title).

Beyond these general suggestions about lists, remember that there are specific considerations that should be made such as type of product, price, and source of funding.

The Offer

A good offer should leave buyers with the feeling that they must act today. More than an invitation to buy, a good offer is an incentive to purchase and is absolutely vital to any successful mailing.

While offers have numerous dimensions, the major components are listed on the next page.

Offer Components

> Price (discount)
> Premium (free gift)
> Means of Payment (cash or credit)
> Conditions of Sale (guarantee)
> Expiration Date

How each of these components is used in combination with others can cause considerable increase (or decrease) in response. One of the golden rules to follow when creating an offer is to keep it simple. It should be instantly easy to understand. If it takes more than a few seconds to derive the benefit of an offer, response may be negatively impacted.

Experience shows that pricing, especially for items of lower value, begins to be attractive at about 20% or more off the suggested retail price. Anything less has not proven to provide significant motivation to respond. Probably the most powerful pricing offer known to man is the half-price or two for the price of one sale.

Premiums can be very effective in developing response. The most important consideration when choosing a premium item is that its perceived value should exceed its actual cost. Respondents should feel they are receiving a free gift that is worth more than its expense to the marketer.

There are, however, a number of considerations when selecting premiums. First, there is the problem of choosing a motivational item.

Selecting items for individual teachers is easier than trying to appeal to a buying committee. When dealing with individuals, the most powerful premiums are those that have classroom as well as home or personal application. Numerous electronic items, books, and desk accessories meet this requirement. When dealing with committee or institutional type purchases, premiums should be more school or classroom oriented.

Another consideration when using premiums is redemption policy. Is the premium automatically shipped with the order, or does the buyer have to redeem it through a coupon, response card, or mention it on a purchase order? If the premium is automatically shipped, it will incur the greatest premium expense but it may also be the most motivational application. If an educator is forced to use a response card or coupon, less premiums will probably be redeemed than if shipment is automatic.

If educators are required to state their premium qualification on the purchase order, this method may not be as effective an incentive. Many educators do not wish to reveal to their school secretaries or business managers that a premium is involved with their order. After all, it may bring their decision to purchase into question within their school community. (A more in-depth discussion regarding premiums can be found in Chapter 6.)

Cash Or Credit

Few subjects can generate the kind of controversy among school marketers as the issue of whether to use a cash or credit offer. Strange as it may seem, the decision is really a function of list selection. It is gener-

ally preferred that a powerful credit offer be made to a select and qualified list rather than making a cash offer to the universe.

School marketers are uniquely fortunate to have a number of factors in
their favor regarding credit. An educator's school name must be supplied before credit is issued. Slow paying teachers can be motivated by
intimating that their administration may be involved to resolve past due
accounts. But the main advantage of the school market compared to
numerous other markets is that teachers and schools are better than
average at paying their bills.

Many individuals complain that schools are notoriously slow payers.
This is a collection problem, not a marketing problem, and is better
solved using modern collection procedures such as repeat billings and
dunning letters. However, slow payment is usually a function of the
bureaucratic accounting procedures found within schools. The question is not *if* payment will be received but rather *when* it will arrive.

Absolutely No Risk

To survive in the mail order business, products must be guaranteed. It
is possible to choose from numerous guarantees and many guarantee
time periods. Interestingly, experience shows that a guarantee will
make little difference once a sale takes place. Those customers who are
dissatisfied will return the product and complain regardless of the guarantee stated in the promotion they received. Remember, the guarantee
is stated in the promotion piece which will probably not be retained for
reference by the time the product arrives. So while it is a strong moti-
vator to purchase, its effects are reduced as time passes.

Why, then, do some marketers detract from their guarantees with limits which make them unattractive? For example, 10-day or even 30-day guarantees are no incentive to educators who order in the spring. Their product usually arrives in August and the guarantee has expired before they've even seen the product.

Keep in mind that the terms of a guarantee do not significantly vary returns or complaints. Also, the prudent marketer will attempt to try to resolve complaints regardless of the guarantee conditions as it is a golden opportunity to develop a lifelong customer.

An effective guarantee is as follows:

Use this fine product in your classroom for one full year. If, at the end of that time, you don't believe it was well worth every penny you paid, return it with a note of explanation. You'll receive a prompt refund or credit for the full purchase price — no questions asked!
Signed,
The President

There are two reasons this guarantee is preferred. First, it doesn't alter the number of complaints or returns that are received. The relationship between sales and returns remains constant. However, it does increase sales. Second, it completely eliminates any concerns the school may have about the vendor.

"You Must Act Today!"

Consumer direct marketers find that these words coupled with a 30- or 60-day expiration date lift their response rates considerably. After all,

expiration dates give credibility to offers and make them truly "special." But perhaps even more important, expiration dates give respondents the reason to act immediately on an offer and not set it aside for
later consideration.

But the school market poses challenges to the use of expiration dates
— especially regarding institutional (purchase order) purchases. This
is particularly true of spring promotions mailed any time from January
through April. A promotion mailed at this time can be destroyed by a
30- to 60-day expiration date, simply because the purchasing bureaucracy cannot accommodate the time limit.

Consider a late August expiration date for spring mailings. It is possible that this extended date may seriously compromise the effectiveness
of the expiration date.   On the other hand, the initiator of the purchase
may deduce that the purchase order will not be issued in time to accommodate an earlier date. Unless such a lengthy date is applied, a considerable amount of institutionally funded response may be discour-
aged.

In the fall, on the other hand, there is no such problem. Mailings that
are released from August through early September can effectively use
an expiration of late October and capture virtually all potential institutional sales. In this time period, budgets are released and spending is
relatively uninhibited.

Format: Response By The Pound

Promotion format refers to the physical characteristics of a mailing. Is it large or small? one piece or many components? light or heavy? and so forth. Few have ever discarded a mailing that weighed close to a pound without some investigation . This is an application of using formats to create interest and, hopefully, response.

The following ranking of promotion formats indicates their potential to generate response.

Ranking	Format	Characteristic
1	Catalog	Minimum 16 pages
2	Direct Mail	Minimum 3 package inserts (letter, brochure, response device)
3	Selfmailer	Any single piece of paper
4	Space Ad	Solicits order or inquiry

As implied in this ranking, some formats have a greater potential to pull more response than others. For example, the catalog is probably the strongest form of direct mail that exists. It can also be the most expensive. Consequently, when selecting the appropriate mailing format, one must weigh the pulling potential of a format against its estimated cost per order.

The trick to selecting an optimal format for a product line involves finding the right blend of format (which ultimately translates to order cost) and response (which ultimately translates to revenue and contribution to promotion, overhead, and profit). Naturally, it is preferable to have some idea of how this relationship will develop before investing in the mail.

A Word Of Caution!

One of the dangers in testing new formats results from lack of expertise in implementing a new style. There is a tendency for creative people who work exclusively with one format to use the same creative approaches on others with disappointing results. For example, people who work consistently with selfmailers sometimes simply substitute the selfmailer for the brochure in a new direct mail package. The letter and order device are added to complete the package and to bring out additional features of the product or offer.

This approach usually isn't very effective. A selfmailer contains far more information than is necessary for a direct mail package brochure — most notably, the entire order device. The premise of a direct mail package is not necessarily to provide more information about products and services. Its function is to present the same basic message in several different ways in order to appeal to a broader base of readers.

Whiz-bangs, Gizmos, And Lumps

One last point should be mentioned before leaving the discussion of promotion formats. That is the use of response lifting devices that are commonly referred to as whiz-bangs, gizmos, and lumps.

Examples of these devices include such items as seals on catalogs, die cuts on order devices, and inserted items (pencils, buttons) in direct mail packages. One popular approach is to simulate the appearance of a handwritten note paper clipped to the cover of a selfmailer or catalog. One mailer actually paper clipped a handwritten note to a selfmailer and reported a very impressive increase in response.

These "gimmicks" add expense to a promotion, but they lift response as well. A direct mail package containing an unknown lump intrigues the recipient and results in an increase in envelopes opened. The same is true for buttons and seals when they're used in an intriguing way. In the school market where so much mail hits simultaneously, it's just one more technique that can be used to make a promotion stand out in the crowd.

Getting Personal For Better Response

School marketers are often embroiled in debate over the use of personal names as opposed to title-addressed mail while consumer mailers seldom debate this issue. Over the years through test after test most consumer mailers are agreed that addressing by name is superior to title. Their only debate centers on the proper degree of personalization. To consumer mailers, it's not so much an issue of whether or not to use a name but how it should be used.

What Is Personalization

The dictionary states that personalization means "to make personal; to have marked with one's initials, name, or monogram." As the dictionary implies and as most consumer direct marketers would add, personalization goes far beyond using a name instead of a title.

The two basic forms of personalization are formal and promotional. Formal personalization includes letters that are generated to address the specifics of a given individual or institution. Those specifics can vary from simply name and address to include information gathered from a database, directory, personal sales call, or telephone discussion.

Formal personalization is ultimately basic business correspondence. It can include handwritten notes in the margin of a letter or response device, check marks to indicate where a person should sign, or use of a second color to highlight or emphasize a point or to draw attention to a feature.

Promotional personalization employs techniques such as laser printing in order to generate a name on an envelope, letter, or response device that may be unusually large in type size for added impact. It also includes gimmicks like personalized stickers or name imprinted pens and pencils. Promotional personalization is limited only by the imagination of the advertiser and the budget of the mailer.

Why Personalize?

Marketers of high ticket items such as an expensive computer system, a consulting service, or even a textbook series, have found that formal personalization pays in many instances. It is often possible to get a far more cost-effective return on a mailing by investing the time and expense in a formal, businesslike personalized communication.

Some educational marketers, particularly those in the juvenile publishing field, have found that promotional personalization also improves results. While the promotion expense is greater, so is the return. When the increase in return is greater than the increase in expense, a lower cost per order can be the result.

Personalization Methods

Most formal personalization is done on a personal computer. Software programs exist that allow a letter outline to be established as one file and a list of the items to be personalized as a second file. The outline file then accesses the file with the personalized data to create the letters.

The major technological device for promotional personalization is the laser printer. A laser printer can generate various type styles and sizes and can also reproduce graphics with typeset quality. Laser printers print on continuous form paper and are capable of running at high speeds and generating large volumes.

The marketer provides a vendor with a mailing list and whatever personal data is to be included in the correspondence in magnetic tape form. The laser printer then writes a program to meet the promotion's specifications and prints the piece.

Making Use Of A Name

Ironically, it is in the school market where the least amount of personalization is attempted that the greatest amount of data exists. Through education data bases, one could create a letter to a school principal or computer coordinator by name, and refer to the quantity and brand of computers in the school. In fact, there are dozens and dozens of pieces of information about schools and various personnel available to school marketers to make interesting, compelling use of both formal and promotional personalization.

To date, most school marketers have simply wrestled with the issue of name versus title. As the competition in the market heats up, views regarding this technique will be expanded. It's time to make use of the names available and the tremendous amount of information that can be obtained with those names. Personalization is a very promising next step.

There are no hard and fast rules when developing a successful promotion. In fact, the possibilities are endless. The most important rule to keep in mind is that a successful promotion generates a profitable return on the investment. Always determine what a promotion will cost prior to its creation. Then determine what response will be necessary for its success. Modify the mailing until both cost and necessary response are within acceptable parameters.

CHAPTER 6

PUMP UP PROFITS WITH PREMIUMS

MENTION PREMIUMS TO educational marketers and you're likely to elicit one of three basic responses: enthusiasm, indifference, or loathing. There are those marketers who enthusiastically endorse the use of premiums because they have seen the positive impact premiums have had on their business. Then there are those fence-sitters who have often toyed with the idea of using premium incentives but, for one reason or another, have not yet taken the plunge. And finally, there are those marketers that strongly object to the idea of including a free gift in any promotion. They feel it degrades their product or service and is an insult to the educator.

Success Stories

There is no doubt that the use of premiums or free gifts can increase response. In fact, given an appealing product or service, experience has shown that including a premium in an offer will almost always generate more response than that identical offer mailed under identical circumstances without a premium. Following are just a few examples of the actual impact premiums have had in a variety of school market situations:

- A book distributor introduced a premium structure in a catalog and increased response by almost 30%.

- A software distributor saw a 20% lift in response after introducing a premium structure in a catalog.

- A video producer gave away a premium with every 30-day trial and increased response by 25%.

- A library marketer promoting high ticket items of about $1500 to school librarians increased business by about one third using premium incentives.

How Much Can You Afford?

There are very few situations where offering a premium would not be appropriate. The trick is finding the right premium(s) for a particular product or promotion. The first step in this process is determining the premium budget.

Introducing a premium item into an offer will add expense. However, the expense should be offset by an increase in response, and/or order size. Therefore, to determine a premium budget, it is necessary to determine what rate of response will be necessary to compensate for the increased cost. Then decide whether or not the increase is realistic.

What Does It Take To Be A Premium

Once a premium budget has been established, the next step is to select an item or items. There are several basic attributes that a premium item should have. While they are all important, these attributes should add up to one important characteristic. A premium should be motivational. It should entice the prospect to investigate a mailing, product or service, and offer, and then encourage them to take the desired action. The trick is finding a premium item that's right for a particular customer.

Begin by envisioning a clear picture of the potential customers. Try to imagine what makes them tick and what might motivate them to act. While a calculator would probably work well as a premium item for both a classroom teacher or an administrator, a set of grading stamps would probably not be as much of an incentive for the administrator. Then, keeping the prospect in mind, try to choose items with the following characteristics:

Desirability: Choose an item a prospect would consider desirable and would like to receive. While the desirability factor may increase with an item's cost, a premium does not necessarily have to be expensive to be desirable. A word of caution. Don't confuse unique with motivational. An item doesn't have to be different to be effective. For example, calculators continue to be motivational premium items despite the fact that they are easily available and that every American probably has at least three!

High perceived value: It is advisable that a premium item have a perceived value greater than its cost. A pencil can make an effective mail opening device when inserted as a lumpy item in an envelope. However, the cost of a pencil is pretty obvious and, despite any enhancements it may have, its perceived value is fairly close to its real cost which can limit its appeal as a premium.

On the other hand, the perceived value of the $4.00 calculator that retails for as much as $15.95 can serve as a strong incentive, especially when promoting relatively low ticket items. Imagine how impressed a customer would be to receive a free item valued at $15.95 with an order for just $25.00!

Attractiveness: While it may go without saying that a premium should be attractive, keep in mind that this attractiveness should be clearly represented in the promotion as well as apparent to the recipient. Many items that appear glamorous in a photo leave something to be desired in real life and vise versa. Choose items that will not only appear attractive in the promotion, but will not disappoint the recipient when they arrive.

While not much can be done to alter the actual appearance of an item, there are methods to honestly enhance appearance for promotion purposes. For example, a set of grading stamps can be photographed with more appeal if a few are shown in use. A pair of book ends would show nicely if they are supporting some colorful books. However, be sure to identify in the promotion materials any items that are shown but are not part of the free gift.

Durability: Make sure items are of an acceptable quality. Be sure to send for samples to review before deciding to promote an item to 10,000 of your best customers. Even if it comes as a free gift, an item of poor quality will create a negative impact on image and reliability. While the response to the initial promotion may be good, subsequent business can be adversely effected.

What's Different About Teacher Premiums

Teachers are no different than anyone else and can be moved to respond with the same types of free gift items as the rest of the world. Teacher premiums should be something the teacher would like to receive as an individual. But in addition, a premium for the education market should also be an item that can be considered appropriate for use in the grade level or subject area at which the promotion is aimed. For example, teachers must feel comfortable about accepting a gift that will benefit their students, even if they are secretly dying to use the premium themselves.

A good example is a camera. Not too many would say "no" to receiving a 35mm camera as a free gift, teachers included. But in addition to making a good premium in the consumer market, a 35mm camera can be used by a teacher to record class field trips or special events and projects. Although it may not be readily associated with classroom use, the camera makes a great teacher premium because it has both classroom and personal appeal.

A word of caution. Under no circumstances should a teacher premium be misconstrued as a bribe. For example, a trip to the Bahamas for the purchasing agent that buys $5,000 worth of computer equipment is not

recommended since it is something from which only the agent will benefit, not the school or district. However, free shipping or free software
appropriate for school use would be perfectly acceptable.

Product Related vs Non Related Premiums

Another question frequently asked regarding premiums is whether a
product related premium produces better results than one that is not
related. This really depends on the situation but a rule of thumb is that
committees respond best to product related premiums while individuals respond best to premiums that are not product related. Another
view expressed by the late direct marketing consultant Jim Benson is
that the desirability of the premium is more important than its relationship to the product.

For example, suppose giving away a free poster with every order for 30
workbooks is attractive because the poster results in only $.42 per item
in premium expense. There are a variety of non product related items
that range in price from $1.00 to $1.50 whose perceived values would
probably produce better results despite the slight increase in premium
cost. However, a purchasing committee considering classroom desks
would probably be better motivated with free freight rather than an
unrelated premium item.

On the other hand, the perfect premium may be in the product line.
Books for either students or teachers, posters, videos, teacher's guides,
and software all make perfectly appropriate classroom gifts. And
often, as mentioned, these types of items can be very cost effective if
they are coming from a company's own inventory. However, don't

consider using premiums as a great way to dispose of excess inventory and obsolete product. Remember, premiums should be attractive and motivational. If the item didn't sell, it probably won't be much of an enticement as a free gift.

There are methods that can be applied to slow moving stock. For example, perhaps paste is overstocked or being discontinued. Consider the "Two For" approach and offer a free jar of paste with every jar ordered.

If the goal is to increase the size of each order, an offer could be created that gives away a free gift for a certain dollar amount or quantity purchased. This redemption requirement should be based on a realistic increase in the most frequent order size or amount.

Perhaps a new product is being introduced. Consider giving away an established and recognized product as an incentive to try the new product.

Discount vs Premium

Are discounts the same as premiums? The answer is no. While discounts can also encourage response, experience shows that they don't always offer the same motivation as a premium.

A discount is a specific, quantifiable number, whether expressed in dollars or percentage of total cost. A premium, on the other hand, usually has a perceived value that may be much greater than its actual cost. For example, consider the calculator that can cost as little as $4.00 but can retail for as much as $15.95. Whereas it may be impossible to offer a discount of $16.00 off the price of a product, giving away a $4.00 premium may be feasible. Conversely, the incentive to respond to an offer that gives away an item valued at $15.95 should be greater than that of a $4.00 discount.

There are, of course, exceptions to the "premium is better than discount" rule. If the decision to purchase is being made by a group or committee, a discount may be more motivational. Offering a premium introduces the dilemma of who in the group will receive the item while a discount can benefit everyone involved. Also, decisions of this type are usually made when purchasing high ticket items where a discount can result in substantial savings.

Premium Structures Improve Catalog Results

A premium structure offering a premium based on the size of an order can produce improved results in a catalog mailing. The purpose of the premium structure is twofold: To increase the size of each order as well as increase the number of orders received.

Unfortunately, catalog marketers often use an average order amount to determine the point at which to offer a free gift. While average order size may be a meaningful way to measure the progress of a business, it is a dangerous number to use when developing marketing strategies.

For example, an average order of $50 is made up of many $20 orders and a few $200 orders. Marketing strategies based on an average of $50 is meaningless to both of these groups. In order to develop an effective premium structure, the price points at which orders tend to cluster should be determined. This can be accomplished by preparing a cluster analysis.

To prepare a cluster analysis, randomly select approximately 200 orders. Mark off a line with meaningful dollar denominations. If products are sold for $20 each, use increments of $20; if products are sold for $1 each, use increments of $1 or $5. Then place a dot above the line at the value of each of the 200 orders. When the analysis is completed, 3 or 4 clusters where the marketplace naturally orders will probably be revealed. These are the price points around which to develop the premium structure.

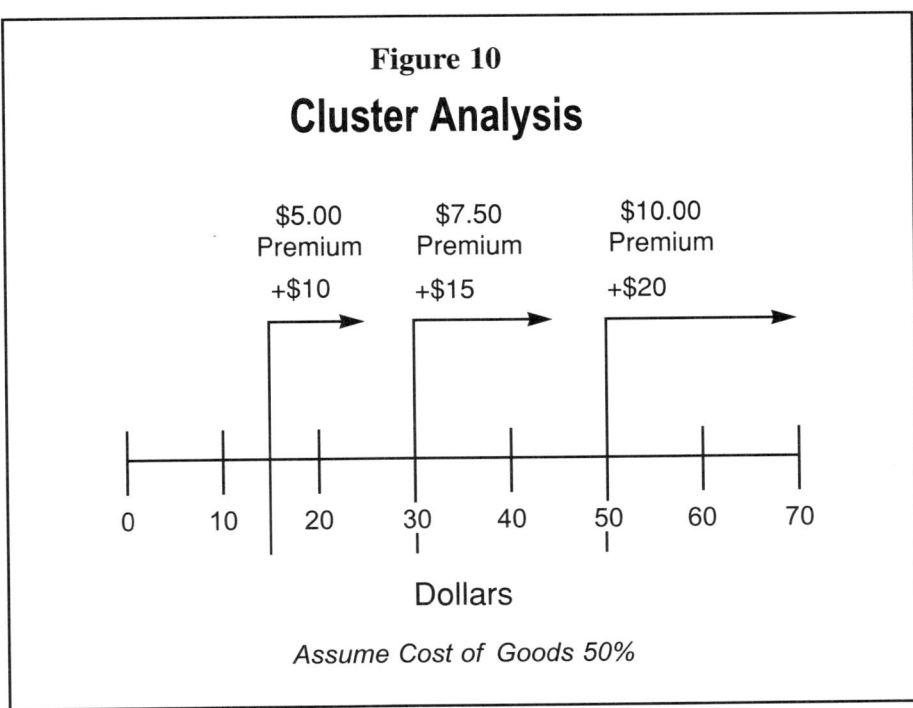

Figure 10

Cluster Analysis

Figure 10 shows an example of a cluster analysis where orders clustered around $15, $30, and $50. The marketing strategy is to increase the $15 orders by $10, increase the $30 orders by $15, and increase the $50 orders by $20. To that end, a premium is offered at the following levels:

> Item A for orders from $25 to $44.99
> Item B for orders from $45 to $69.99
> Item C for orders $70 or more

Assuming a cost of goods at 50% and based on the order increase forecast, premium A's cost should be $5, $7.50 for premium B, and $10 for premium C.

If a premium structure is effective, the points at which the orders cluster should be increasing with time. Therefore, a cluster analysis should be completed each year to determine if the redemption levels should be modified. With time, a limit will probably be reached beyond which order amounts cannot be increased. This is another important piece of information that can be revealed through a cluster analysis.

Does It Pay To Pay For Previews?

Some school marketers have offered premiums in return for a product preview regardless of whether or not the preview leads to a purchase. Is this a bold stroke of marketing savvy or a blind retaliation to frightening sales statistics?

The case for giving premiums for previews is based upon the belief that there is a relatively constant relationship between the number of previews and sales. If for every 10 previews there are 2 sales, and this relationship holds constant, then it follows that if the number of previews is increased, the number of sales will also increase.

Assuming this theory is true, then the expense of the premium may be evaluated against the increase in previews and sales and its effect on net sales. If the incremental increase in net sales is greater than the premium expense, it's generally considered a success.

Most audio visual materials enjoy a relationship between cost of goods and selling price that is advantageous to the application of premiums. Let's assume a product sells for $100 with a $30 production cost (never put the pressure of recovering development costs on an incremental sales concept like premium usage). Every time a unit is sold, $70 is contributed toward the cost of promotion (including premiums), overhead, and profit. In this example, if a $2 premium is offered, only a 2.9% increase in net sales needs to be realized to recover the premium expense. A $5 premium would require a 7% increase in response and a $10 premium a 14% increase in response.

Premiums at these various cost points might include:

Premium Budget	Item
$2.00	Sport watch
$5.00	Calculator or pocket data bank
$10.00	Clock radio or personal stereo cassette player

Reaching a final decision regarding which premium item to offer is a difficult compromise at best. For example, the sport watch is least expensive and needs to generate the least increase in percent response to break even. Yet, the watch may also be the least attractive of the three items.

On the other hand, the clock radio or cassette player at $10 may be so attractive as to draw response simply to get the free gift. Thus, the increase in preview response may not yield the anticipated constant rate of conversion to sales.

The calculator or data bank at $5 may be the best choice. It's promotionally attractive, yet not so attractive as to draw poor quality preview requests. Conversely, it may be just attractive enough to generate the necessary increase in preview requests.

Promote Premiums Prominently

There's little question that adding premiums increases the power of a promotion piece. If the free gift is motivational, most people take the time to learn what they have to do in order to receive the gift. This begins the process of involvement with the promotion. As a rule, when involvement and readership are increased, response is increased as well.

Another rule of thumb regarding premiums is that half of a premium's effectiveness stems from the item itself. The other half is a result of how well the premium is promoted. Don't hide the fact that a free gift is being offered. Highlight the gift on the outer envelope of a direct mail package, on the front and/or back cover of a catalog, or on the first panel(s) the recipient will see on a self-mailer. Repeat the information throughout the promotion, particularly on or near the order device.

Also, make sure the premium is shown to its best advantage. If a desk organizer is offered, fill it with colorful pens, pencils, push pins, note paper, etc. to enhance its appeal. However, as previously stated in this chapter, if items are being added in a premium photo that are not included with the free item, make sure to state this in the promotion.

Do Premiums Hurt A Company's Image?

Many educational marketers are concerned that using premiums will hurt their image in the marketplace. However, if this was true, premiums would probably not be used so extensively.

Take a look at the competition. If they are using premiums, chances are premiums are improving their results. Of course, the next step would be to test the use of premiums. The issue is really the bottom line and what premiums can do to enhance profitability. Testing is ultimately the only way to determine the effectiveness of premiums for a particular situation.

To ease their conscience, some marketers mix some more education-oriented premiums in with what might be considered less conventional items. For example, a choice of either a calculator or a set of classroom books may be offered.

The Case Against Premiums

There are two arguments against premiums. One is that using premiums causes customers to become "premium conditioned." Then, if circumstances cause premiums to be withdrawn from future offers, this conditioning causes a significant decline in sales.

While this notion of "premium conditioning" is acceptable, it should not totally rule out the use of premiums. If the premium increases sales at an acceptable cost per order, who cares if customers have been "premium conditioned?"

The second argument is the premise that using premiums causes educators to believe that prices must be artificially increased to cover the cost of the premium. While some percentage of the marketplace adheres to this premise, it is believed that they are in the minority. If a premium causes the desired sales increase at an acceptable cost per order, let the minority of educators believe what they will.

Coming To A Decision

Deciding the issue of premiums is very difficult. It's difficult because getting a good reading requires considerable time and patience.

One successful technique that can be employed is to split a mailing between odd and even sectional centers or zip codes. Mail a premium offer to one group and the non premium or "control" offer to the other. Continue this approach for a period of two years and check the results at the end of each year. Then, after the two year period is up, make a decision regarding the use of premiums based on actual test results.

One note of caution. Be sure to use a premium item that is proven to be successful, not one that Aunt Mary or a neighbor has chosen. The trick is to keep the premium itself from being a variable in the test.

At the end of the two years, compare total sales in one group with those of the other. Deduct the total promotion expense for both groups, including the premium expense in the premium test group, and evaluate the resulting contributions to overhead and profit. It's seldom a close call.

Premium Pitfalls: Let The Buyer Beware

Premium procurement can be a challenging responsibility, particularly in the education market. Educational marketers mail at very precise times of the year. It is critical that premiums be shipped in a timely fashion, not only because this is a prudent fulfillment policy, but because product and premiums must be received before schools close. Be sure to verify availability and lead times. Many premium items are manufactured overseas. Find out if the importer keeps inventory stocked in the U.S. should additional items be required. Otherwise a wait of 60 to 90 days for a ship to arrive from Asia may occur.

Pricing can be difficult because many items are volume sensitive. When quoted a price, be sure to ask to what quantities a particular price applies and where price breaks occur. Also, inquire as to minimum purchase quantities; what, if any, case quantities apply; and if there are penalties for purchasing other than case quantities.

Often it takes time to establish credit with a premium supplier. They may want cash with a first order before establishing credit terms. If large quantities are being purchased, the vendor may require a domestic or foreign letter of credit.

Get out there. Attending premium or merchandise trade shows is a good idea. It's wise to gather as much information as practical in order to locate alternative sources to interesting items. Then, if prices change or availability on items fluctuates, alternative supplies can be quickly found.

Pre-select some items. Have an idea of what may be appropriate for a product and program as well as a price range and estimated quantity that might be required. Taking a look at what the competition is using can be a good source of ideas. Frankly, in general, the types of premium items used by educational marketers don't vary too much year to year. But price, features, and availability can.

Trade shows are usually large and can be overwhelming. Having potential items in mind prior to arrival makes it possible to select exhibitors to visit from the directory that is usually provided at registration. This directory is an invaluable reference tool to use when premium shopping. It alphabetically lists all exhibitors at the show, their addresses, phone numbers, key personnel and a list of items the company carries. In addition, the directory includes a section that groups exhibitors by the category of product they carry. Be alert for new ideas as well. And be sure to wear comfortable shoes!

Ask questions. There are some key questions that should be answered when sourcing premiums. Cost, of course, is key. Very often cost is determined by quantity so, as mentioned before, it's helpful to have that information. Find out if freight charges are included in the quoted price and how long the price is guaranteed. If drop-shipping is required, ask if that is available and what must be provided to the vendor. Be sure to get the name of the person providing the information and take notes for later reference.

Unlike retailers or consumer marketers, many education marketers must select items well in advance of their actual mailing. Ask about availability. Is it warehoused in the U.S. or imported? Will it be available when it's needed five months from the show and will the price be the same? What kind of lead time is recommended for placing an order to ensure timely receipt of the item? If the quantity is misjudged and more items are required, will small quantities (a couple of hundred) be available quickly? What is the policy on returns and/or damaged items? How can credit be established?

Many school marketers are enthusiastically using premiums to their advantage. For those marketers who are either opposed to using premiums or still riding the fence, take a look at the competition. If they have incorporated premiums into their offers, chances are premiums could improve your results as well. Consider testing the concept in your next promotion.

CHAPTER 7

BETTER COPYWRITING AND DESIGN

MANY OF THOSE involved in the promotion cycle of companies spend the majority of their time planning and executing the copy and design of the promotions. It's interesting to note, however, that copy and art contribute less to response than do list selection, offer creation, format selection, and timing. Still, the promotion is the vehicle through which offers are communicated to both existing and potential customers. To assume it is unimportant would be a major miscalculation.

Keep in mind, however, that even the most expensive and award-winning design can't compensate for poor list selection, lack of product appeal, or a bad offer. Proper list selection, a quality product, and a strong offer must also be present if a promotion effort is to succeed.

The method used to create a direct mail promotion can be as varied as the individual(s) involved in the creative process. There are, however, guidelines of which one should be aware prior to embarking on this challenging and exciting endeavor. This chapter will serve as a general guide of useful tips to aid in the successful completion of your next creative process.

Develop an Attitude

Designing promotion pieces can appear to be a grueling experience. There can be nothing more intimidating than that blank piece of paper or computer screen just daring you to make your first tentative creative move. Compound this "designer's block" with a tight budget and the task can take on Herculean dimensions. However, there are some ways to overcome a limited promotion budget and create an attractive, interesting, and inspiring promotion piece that will accomplish your marketing objectives.

When working creatively, attitude has a great deal to do with the outcome of the finished product. Given the responsibility of creating an attractive, appealing, eye-catching promotion piece that sells can be overwhelming. But the better one feels about the project, the greater the chance of achieving the project's goals. Begin by taking a positive approach and think of the creative process as an exciting challenge with endless possibilities.

Getting Started

Each promotion should have one main theme which should be carried through all pieces contained in the project. The theme should be something unique or outstanding that will encourage readership and motivate the reader to take the desired action. It can be based on the offer, product, or service. For example, a savings of 50%, a product designed to eliminate lesson planning, or the fact that shipments are mailed 12 hours after receiving an order are significant, motivating benefits with which prospects can identify. Any one or combination of these benefits would make a good basis on which to build a creative approach.

Brainstorming can be helpful when trying to determine a promotion theme. And while it is always helpful to have the input of others, brainstorming can be just as effective when done on an individual basis. After reviewing the product and offer, write down everything that comes to mind including headlines, subheads, graphics, and lines of copy for any and all pieces contained in the promotion. Include everything, no matter how trivial or ridiculous it may seem. Not only can the ridiculous sometimes trigger a brilliant idea, it makes for some fun during the process and can help to create a positive outlook toward the project.

If possible, sleep on the ideas expressed in the brainstorming session in order to give them the "morning after" test. Time can sometimes have a significant effect on the way in which creative options are viewed.

Once a main theme has been determined, don't discard any notes. Other items that might have been recorded during the brainstorming sessions may also be significant and could be included somewhere in the promotion.

Organizing The Layout

After a promotion theme has been determined, the next step is to decide what goes where. This can become a rather complicated process and can vary for different promotion formats. However, regardless of the format, begin with a blank mock-up of the piece either in actual size or in a reduced form called thumbnails. Then allocate space and note in general what is to appear in each area. Remember, this is a *rough* (the operative word) indication of what will appear in each piece, not a comprehensive or finished layout.

As mentioned, allocating space can become a rather complicated process. Following are some guidelines regarding space allocation for four major types of promotion formats:

Catalogs: The most important pages are those that are seen first and include front cover, back cover, front inside spread (pages 2 and 3), center spread (middle two pages in a saddle-stitched catalog), back inside spread (last two pages) and the order form. Motivational information such as new products, best sellers, special offers, guarantees, toll free numbers, and free items should appear in these areas. An index can appear on page 2 or 3.

The remainder of the space should be allocated to product based on sales history. For example, let's assume the catalog contains 64 pages. After filling the covers, pages 2 and 3 (first spread), pages 62 and 63 (last spread), and pages 31 and 32 (the center spread), there are 56 pages remaining. If product 4 generates 12% of the sales, then it should be allocated 12% of the remaining space or 6 3/4 pages.

It is important to keep in mind, however, that this procedure is a guideline. Judgment, common sense, and intuition also play a role when allocating space. Very few products require 6 3/4 pages of catalog space so it will probably be necessary to reduce the allocation of pages needed for product 4.

On the other hand, product 400 may only generate enough sales to merit a few square inches of space. While the space allocated to it should be minimal, it must be at least enough to allow those interested to correctly understand and order the product. A more in depth discussion of planning a catalog may be found in Chapter 5.

Direct Mail Package:

Envelope - A good place for teaser copy regarding the theme of the promotion (i.e., special offer, discount, free gift, etc.). It may also include interesting graphics. Remember, the envelope's job is to generate enough interest to get opened and entice the reader inside.

Brochure - The brochure is the visual rendition of the sales message so keep copy at a minimum and focus on a more graphics-oriented explanation. It should contain all elements covered in the promotion in a condensed form. Important points should be highlighted on front and back covers. Back cover can include guarantee, toll free number, testimonials, offer information, brief description of company, the product's creator or author, and/or instructions on how to order if the order form is missing. In addition to product explanation, the inside spread should contain key points such as offer information, free gift, or description of special savings.

Letter - The letter is the narrative rendition of the message so don't be afraid to be wordy. Include description of product, offer information highlighting special savings, free gift description, guarantee information, and/or toll free numbers. Be sure to add a P.S. message. A headline or script message on the first page focusing on the theme of the mailing can encourage readership.

Order Form - The order form is the concise, abbreviated version of the message. Keep it brief and to the point. Include "Ship To" and "Bill To" address, contract copy stating terms of the offer, phone number for questions or to order, area to indicate product selections if applicable, return address, toll free numbers, easy ordering instructions, and/or free gift information.

Other components could include a flyer, publisher's note (lift letter), postage-paid return envelope, product sampling, and/or a free item such as stickers, pencil, poster, or a list of "15 Time-Saving Teacher Tips".

Selfmailer: Layout can be similar to a brochure in the sense that it should be visually oriented with sparse copy. However, since this is the only promotion piece, it must contain complete information regarding the product or service, offer, and how to order. If generating an order or response is the purpose of the selfmailer, remember to include a response device preferably located on the inside back cover. A mailing area with room for a label, return address, and indicia must also be included.

Space Ad: When possible, graphics should dominate with copy held to a minimum. In those cases where graphics are not applicable, include attention-getting, provocative headlines and copy. If needed, include a response device where it can be easily detached such as the lower righthand corner. This is probably the least structured form of direct response advertising in the sense that the only creative limit is the size of the ad.

Each one of these formats along with proper allocation of space is discussed in more detail in subsequent chapters.

Inspired Graphics

Graphics is an important aspect of almost every type of direct response promotion. It is one of the most effective ways of capturing interest and readership. Graphics can visually stimulate the reader, can be used to highlight an important point or feature, and can serve to illustrate the product and/or its use(s). They set the tone for the message and create a mood to the mailing. This can range from deadly serious or dramatic to somewhat urgent or even lightheartedly funny. Even in the creation of letters and envelopes, graphics can have an important place.

If money is no object, elaborate scenes on location can be staged during photography sessions along with the use of 4-color processing, expensive stock for printing as well as a variety of other eye-catching but costly techniques. However, more often than not budget restrictions make it necessary to keep the cost of implementing creative ideas a major concern.

Incorporating motivational graphics doesn't necessarily mean spending megabucks on models and photography. Often inspiring graphics are ready-made right at your fingertips for little or no cost. For example, many times the product can supply graphics for a piece. The illustrations from a book, slides from an audio visual program, or existing art from a previous promotion are all good, economical sources for graphics.

Perhaps the product has other aspects that could be used as graphics. For instance, artwork created for the product itself or for product packaging can be a very economical source of illustration. And it can convey an accurate representation of the product for the reader.

Clip-art is artwork created specifically for reuse and provides an economical graphic alternative. Clip art can be purchased in electronic or hard copy form either on a one-time or subscription basis. And it may be purchased by category such as seasons, computer equipment, family scenes, or borders, along with a multitude of other choices. The cost of clip-art books, software, and subscriptions is minimal when compared to the hundreds of graphics that will be received that can be mixed and matched or used individually. Because they are "stock" illustrations, the challenge comes in blending them into a specific promotion concept.

A Picture Is Worth A Thousand Words

Photography can do a great deal to enhance the readership a promotion generates, and greater readership can lead to more orders. But photography can be a very expensive undertaking if it isn't carefully considered and planned for. Here are some helpful tips to keep in mind when planning a photo session.

Tips For Better Product Shots

Tip No. 1 Do All The Photography At One Time

When planning to photograph several different products individually, try to deliver them to the photographer so they can all be photographed at one time rather than piecemeal. This will reduce the photographer's time, materials, and, ultimately, the cost.

Tip No. 2 Group Products Together

Consider grouping products rather than shooting them individually. For example, if five different books are being offered together in a set, consider one photograph of all five books rather than five different shots of one book each. This approach eliminates the cost of four additional shots.

However, if there's a chance two of the five books may be replaced in future promotions, it may be more cost effective in the long run to photograph the books individually. That way existing individual photos can be mixed and matched to create different sets and the need for new photos is limited.

Another option could be to take a group shot but avoid overlapping product. Then it is sometimes possible to eliminate old product and strip in photographs of new items.

Tip No. 3   Pay Attention To Detail

Pay attention to detail. If photographing a black and white shot of a book with a white cover - don't shoot it on a light gray background because the book will blend in and become lost. The exception would be if the book is to be silhouetted (elimination of the background). If silhouetting is the goal, then the background should be very light for best results.

Pay attention to detail. If students are supposed to be working at their desks with workbooks they should have pencils in hand. Don't be afraid to ask models to straighten a tie or smooth their hair. Make sure that telephone book on which the model is sitting to add height will be hidden in the final shot.

Tip No. 4   Add A Personal Touch

Add interest to product shots. For example, if photographing a bulletin board, tack a few notes on it. Not only will this clearly dramatize the bulletin board's usefulness but it will stimulate interest in the photo - especially if what is written on the notes can be read in the photo.

Blackboards can make great areas on which to place a promotional headline or message. This technique is especially helpful if attempting to highlight a particular point in the promotion piece because almost everyone will read what is written on the blackboard. However, the material may be difficult to read if it is actually written on the board itself and then photographed. Instead, create the message as artwork and crop it into a blank blackboard in the photo during preparation of the final film.

When promoting a software program, don't simply use a photo of a disk. Disks are rather mundane in that they pretty much all look the same. Instead, show a photo of one of the more interesting screens from the program. That photo will not only be more visually appealing, but it can also show the reader what is beneficial or unique about the program.

Other examples would include displaying numbers on a calculator or filling a desk organizer with interesting items. It doesn't take much to enhance some photos. However, it should be made clear to the recipient if there are any items in a photo that are not included with the product.

Tip No. 5   Make Sure The Product Looks Good

Make sure the product looks its best. For example, if a book is being promoted with beautiful four-color illustrations, don't just show the cover of the book. The fact that it's beautifully illustrated is a benefit that can best be shown through a four-color photo of one of the inside illustrations.

Appearance is everything. If there's a smudge, remove it; if there's a wrinkle, iron it; if there's a dent or a crack, don't use it! Impress upon the photographer that if product arrives in a damaged condition it should be replaced. The tiniest flaw can ruin a shot and probably the promotion's results.

Tip No. 6   Show Good Value

When possible, show value in product shots. If a product is boxed, take the product out of the box and display it to clearly show its worth. If the copy that goes with the photo talks about value, the photo should visually support the claim. Show all books in the 10-book set or all 16 workbooks that are included in the classroom set. Volume adds to perceived value.

Tip No. 7   Provide Good Layouts

Be sure to provide the photographer with comprehensive layouts and, if possible, key the product to the layout. For example, use alphabetical indicators such as "A", "B", or "C" on the layout. Then provide a list that explains that "A" indicates a calculator and "B" indicates a pencil sharpener. This is particularly helpful when working with silhouetted or outlined photos as opposed to square-up shots.

By giving photographers comprehensive layouts, they can be sure the angles and perspectives of the actual shots match the layouts and fit with the type and design. Keying product to a layout assumes that the right product is shot correctly the first time, eliminating unnecessary expense.

Another advantage to providing comprehensive layouts is that they enable the photographer to provide correctly sized prints. This will also reduce cost by reducing the amount of photographs requiring resizing by the printer.

Make sure the photographer has a layout so he/she can see the shot exactly as it should appear. In the case of more difficult photos where positioning of copy or other art might be a factor, the photographer can create an outline on tissue of the photo from the layout. By positioning this tissue over the camera lens, it is possible to make sure the shot is executed exactly as the designer has indicated.

Tip No. 8   Include Points Of Reference

Depending on the type of product, it may be preferable to include some way of relating to the product's size. Take the example of exercise mats for elementary school students. In a photo, a rectangular mat could be any size. By placing a student on the mat, one can estimate the relative size of the item easily.

Tips For Staged or "People" Shots

People add interest to photos. People like to look at other people and can identify more easily with product benefits portrayed in real-life situations. People can add spice to a photo in a variety of ways. For example, rather than simply showing people using a product, stage the photo for added interest. This could be accomplished subtly such as using a child with a particularly disarming look or more radically by staging a dramatic scene.

Of course, product can be shown without people in the picture. However, "people" photos are recommended for primary types of shots (i.e., catalog covers, brochure covers, space ads, etc.). Product shots are recommended in secondary types of photos (i.e., inside pages of catalogs or brochures).

Photos that involve people can dramatically increase cost. Once models are included, photography cost estimates must include:

> Model fees
> Agency fees
> Increase in number of shots
> Increase in amount of film
> Increase in photographer's time (fee)

Don't misunderstand. Promotion photos that include people are the preferred choice. They add a whole new dimension of interest and believability and there's probably no better way to encourage readership. However, they also add a new challenge in controlling costs and logistics.

Tip No. 9   Shoot In A Studio

It's much easier to control the photo sessions (and the resulting costs) if the sessions take place in a photographer's studio. It may seem like a good idea to shoot on location, but consider the added difficulties.

Suppose the photography session is planned to take place in an actual classroom. There may be no control over the room selection resulting in a room that does not fit the layout. The teacher may be enthusiastic but simply a terrible model. And after everything is all set up, it is difficult to diplomatically explain to the teacher that she's not providing the facial expression that is needed.

As for the students, anyone who has tried knows it's difficult enough to control one or two youngsters during a photography session even if they're pros. It is almost impossible to control five or ten children who are not experienced models.

Tip No. 10   Sometimes Less Students Are Better

Shots can be staged to give the feeling that there is a full classroom of students beyond the borders of the picture. And in addition to better control of the circumstances, studio shots with one to three students tend to be tighter and, therefore, afford other benefits. For example, if a product is in use, it can be shown more closely and clearly. Special effects such as shocked or surprised expressions can be more dramatically portrayed.

Tip No. 11   Professional Models Yield The Best Results

When shooting photographs for promotions, professional models will produce the best results — especially when children are involved. Professional models are experienced at posing for photographs and are not intimidated by the camera. Professional photos that enhance a promotion will be of a much better quality and much easier to obtain.

Oh sure, little Susie next door may be cute as a button, but put her in front of a camera and she bursts into tears. The additional cost of professional models - both child and adult - is almost always worth the expense. They will most likely save time and provide much better results. And there's another advantage to using professionals. A model who isn't working out can be more diplomatically replaced than someone's next door neighbor and child.

Tip No. 12   Use A Reliable Agency

Find a reliable agency. Most modeling agencies are qualified and professional but it doesn't hurt to shop around for the best price. Be sure to inquire about the agency's fee in addition to the model's hourly rate. Most agencies have models available at different hourly rates. If the rate sounds too high, ask if there is someone available at a lower rate.

Ask two or three agencies to forward their catalog of models. Not only does the catalog make it possible to choose the exact model for a shot, but the agency will have a good idea of the "look" that is needed. It is best to have two or three models in mind in the event the first choice is not available.

Explain to the agency exactly the type of shot(s) that are needed. Models should bring several clean and pressed outfits to make sure they look just right. Remember, most teachers are not nor can they afford to dress on the cutting edge of fashion. Conservative clothing and a minimum amount of makeup is preferable. If the shot is to be silhouetted, avoid a model with curly hair. It will make silhouetting the photo difficult at best.

As children age, their appearance can change very quickly and dramatically. When reviewing photos of children, ask how recently they were taken and the birth date of the child. As a rule of thumb, any photo of a child that is more than six months old probably does not accurately portray the model. This is particularly true of younger children.

Keep a file of preferred agencies and models. A good model is prepared, cooperative, flexible, and helps to make photographs believable!

Tip No. 13   Use A Polaroid Camera

A Polaroid camera is a handy way to get a real sense of how the finished shot will appear. Before wasting a roll of film or an entire photo session, have the photographer shoot a Polaroid and crop it or frame it as it would appear in the promotion. It is much easier and more economical to make last minute adjustments at this stage as opposed to after the film has been processed.

Tip No. 14   Include An Author's Photo

Often a promotion piece may contain information regarding the author, creator, or publisher of a product. If this is the case, try to include a photo of that person. The photo will not only draw the reader to that section, but will create a more personal and intimate atmosphere as well as add to the product's credibility.

Tip No. 15   Consider Stock Photos

Should photo needs be complex, consider the stock photo. There are many stock photo houses that inventory thousands of photos, both full color and black and white, that are available on a rental basis. Usually the company publishes a catalog from which shots may be selected. Or simply contact the company with a description of what is required and they will send a variety of photos for consideration. Stock photos are usually available in several forms including a traditional transparency, on CD-ROM or disk, and via the Internet.

Cost will depend on the type of piece in which the photo will be used, the print quantity, the position and size of the photo, as well as other criteria. While this service is not inexpensive, it can be particularly economical if your needs are fairly complex. For example, the company located in New Mexico can easily obtain a photo of the White House in Washington, D.C without ever leaving the office.

Tip No. 16   Use Captions

Photos should always be captioned when possible. When scanning a direct mail piece, the eye is often drawn to a photo first. If the photo includes a caption, the reader is likely to read the caption next. The caption can cause a very important transition to take place by slowing the scanning process enough to start the recipient reading the promotion copy.

The caption does not necessarily have to describe the visual. For example, by telling the reader a product does more than teach vocabulary without explaining how that is done, the scanner is encouraged to continue reading to gain information on any other benefits the product may include.

In addition to photos, the term graphics also includes illustrations, line art, bursts, and corner cuts. Some of these can be used to draw attention to items such as premiums offered, discounts on products, new products, guarantees, or ordering information.

Line art can be used in place of photos, although there are few cases where it is as effective. Because line art is an artistic rendition of a product or product in use, it is less likely to have the impact that the reality of photography can. In some instances, line art can create skepticism on the part of the reader. The reader may assume the illustration is used to enhance the product's attractiveness and, consequently, it can create a negative product image.

The term graphics can also include type. An unusual or interesting typeface used sparingly is an inexpensive way to generate interest. However, most direct mail promotions are initially quickly scanned. It is best to avoid typefaces and spacing (leading) that is difficult to read or will impede the scanning process.

Script messages are useful ways of stimulating curiosity and interest. A message that appears to be personally directed at the reader can promote a feeling of intimacy and importance. Script messages are especially useful in letters or as teaser copy on envelopes.

Writing Copy

At this point in the creative process, although little consideration has been given to body copy, a basic idea of what to say and where to say it is probably evolving. It goes without saying that copy should be grammatically correct. However, it should also be simple and to the point. The goal is to impart important information concisely and completely, not write the next **War and Peace**. Sentences should be fairly short, heads and subheads brief, and readers should be able to scan each piece and determine those areas in which they are most interested for further investigation.

New Or Free!

The underlying motive for readership in advertising material is self-interest on behalf of an individual or the institution that individual represents. Unless the promotion appeals to this sense of self-interest, readership and, subsequently, response will probably be negatively effected.

When creating copy and design that will captivate scanners, review headlines, subheads, and copy carefully. Two of the most motivational words you can use are *NEW* and *FREE*. Using this simple rule of thumb will help to encourage more readers, and that usually leads to more responses.

Don't worry about repeating information if there is more than one piece in the promotion. Almost every piece should contain all the information that is to be covered. The purpose of a letter is to cover it in detail while the brochure is a more concise, visually-oriented version of the same information. Space ads are much more likely to be scanned quickly and usually contain a minimum of copy.

Envelopes are meant to be opened and covers are meant to be turned. Don't tell the whole story in these locations. Tease with one or two important points that will stimulate enough interest for the reader to investigate further.

Hit 'Em With Your Headline

The rule of thumb that many direct response marketers use when creating most types of promotions is the 10 second time limit. A promotion must capture the readers' attention within 10 seconds. Otherwise the reader is on to the next piece of mail. The best way to generate readership is through graphics, headlines, or a combination of the two.

Following are some guidelines to keep in mind when creating headlines and subheads:

1. Make it short and sweet. Don't try to tell the whole story in the headline. The purpose of a headline is to grab readers' attention and encourage them to read further. If a headline contains more than 10 words, it's probably too long. Keep in mind that subheads may be used to support main headlines and their use will help to keep the length of headlines under control.

2. Give the reader a reason to read. One of the best ways to grab a reader with a headline is to talk about how the reader can benefit from the product. Begin by listing all the benefits the product(s) offers. Examples of some teacher benefits might be less time spent preparing lesson plans, ways to increase student interest, or ways to brighten up a classroom. Administrator benefits might include saving money or ways to make teachers more productive.

After completing a list of benefits, choose the one that is believed will most interest the audience receiving the promotion. That benefit should be the theme of the main headline. Depending on the benefit, the headline may or may not need support from subheads.

Following are some examples of motivational headlines:

Don't say: ***Bob's Math Workbook***

Try: ***Teach Twice The Math With Half The Effort***

Don't say: ***Fraction And Decimal Computer Program***

Try: ***Two Computer Programs For The Price Of One***

Don't say: ***ACME's Educational Catalog***

Try: ***Over 100 Ways To Make Learning Fun****

*This assumes the catalog contains over 100 items.

3. Don't make incredible claims. Direct response buyers are a pretty sophisticated lot. They are not usually impressed by the use of superlatives. As a matter of fact, this approach usually makes the reader wary of the company that makes outlandish claims and discourages response.

If a claim is made in a headline or subhead, make sure it is substantiated in the copy that follows. For example, if a headline states "You Can Save 75%!," make sure an explanation of how that's possible is included by clearly stating the product's value along with the special sale price.

4. Don't use difficult words. Don't assume educators need to be impressed with words that are not easily understood. Always remember that educators are people too, and are influenced by the same types of things as the rest of the population — free gifts, time-saving products, and words that don't have to be looked up in the dictionary. Use words in headlines and subheads that are simple and easy to read.

5. Heads and subheads should make scanning easy. Many people don't like to read very much — especially large blocks of direct mail copy. Therefore, the essence of the message should be evident through the heads and subheads.

Make a list of the main points that are to be covered in the promotion piece. These points should all be highlighted by heads and subheads in such a way that makes them obvious to the reader without having to wade through lengthy body copy. If the reader has questions or wishes to get additional information on a topic, the heads and subheads should make it immediately obvious as to where the reader should look for particular information.

Headlines can't stand alone or work entirely on their own. A successful direct mail piece is a combination of factors. Once a scanner's attention is obtained with a headline, convincing body copy will help stimulate action on the part of the reader.

Beef Up Your Body Copy

Body copy is included in almost all forms of direct response promotion to one degree or another. It's an important part of each promotion piece because, after all, it's usually through the body copy the reader is told important facts about:

- The product(s) capabilities and benefits.
- The details of the offer, such as price, guarantees, length of trial periods, etc.
- Any premiums that may be offered.
- How to order.

The headlines and subheads may have grabbed the reader's attention but it's the body copy that will cement the sale. Here are some do's and don'ts to keep in mind when writing body copy.

Body Copy Do's

1. Direct the copy toward the audience (reader) as specifically as possible. If librarians are the target, talk about features with which they can identify such as increasing traffic in their library. Math teachers might be interested in ways to stimulate student interest or easy methods to evaluate student progress.

If the promotion is going to a diverse group of people, find some interests that would be common to the majority of the group. Or consider modifying the promotion for each group. That is, create several similar promotions by altering the body copy to fit the specific audience.

2. Mention benefits with which the reader can identify! A teacher doesn't want to read about how well a math workbook teaches addition—there are hundreds of math workbooks that can do that. Instead, mention that all the answers are included in the teacher's guide to save them time. Include the fact that there are teaching tips for presenting material that will eliminate lesson planning. Tell teachers what the product can do to make their life easier first. Student benefits should come second.

3. Include specifics about the product. Include the number of pages, size, number of colors, price, and any other pertinent details. Don't leave anything to the reader's imagination. In all purchase decisions the product's value is evaluated so it is important that a complete and precise product description be provided.

4. Use type that is easy to read. The type size for body copy probably should not be less than eight or nine points. Stay **away** from fancy, elaborate type styles. Some designers believe they're attractive and will capture attention, but they will not enhance the promotion's readability.

Body Copy Don'ts

1. Avoid large or deep blocks of text. They are imposing and give the impression that reading the piece will be too much work. Each paragraph should appear easy to read.

There are devices that can limit copy blocks and encourage readability. Try including an interesting subhead between every second or third paragraph. Itemize several items in a list rather than presenting them in paragraph form. These items could be preceded by a number, bullet, or asterisk.

2. Avoid large, complicated words. Copy should be easily under-stood regardless of the fact that it is being received by educators. A good rule of thumb is any word that consists of more than 15 letters is probably too long.

This includes the use of professional terms that may not be easily understood by the layman. For example, a high school science product may explain how some scientists believe the rings around the planet Saturn consist of unaccreted material from the planet's nebular, held in eternal thrall to Saturn's gravity. However, this aspect of the product would be better described as, "includes several scientific theories about the mysterious rings that circle the planet Saturn."

3. Avoid complicated and run-on sentences. Keep sentences short, simple, and to the point. Nothing will cause a reader to lose interest faster than wading through long, difficult sentences.

4. Avoid text that is too wide. Long stretches of copy make it diffi-cult for the reader to pick up the next line of text. Don't be afraid to widen margins and increase white space. This can make copy appear less intimidating and more inviting.

Tantalize With Teaser Copy

Why take the chance that a direct mail package or catalog will be thrown away without being opened or perused? Make prospects open and manipulate a promotion by using teaser copy that intrigues, piques interest, or creates curiosity. The main objective of teaser copy is to draw the prospect into the promotion and begin the momentum that leads to response. Following are some examples:

FREE $10 VALUE *(See Inside)!*

Your Choice Of Valuable Classroom Aids FREE! *(See page 10 for details)*

What's Easy To Use, Motivates Students, and Costs Just Pennies Per Day? *(Answer enclosed)*

Too often, school marketers either use ineffective teaser copy or eliminate it altogether on outer envelopes and catalog covers. This is a wasted opportunity. The cost of printing those envelopes and covers is incurred regardless, so the cost of teaser copy is negligible. However, the effect such copy can have on response can be considerable.

The most powerful teaser copy is usually offer related. "Special Spring Sale," "Two For One," "Free Offer (See Inside)" are all examples of offer related teasers. Teaser copy can also refer to product benefits or attributes.

Catalog marketers to schools are notorious for omitting teaser copy on front and back covers. The traditional catalog cover usually consists of a pretty picture with company logo and possibly a product reference. Teaser copy affords school catalog marketers the opportunity to give the prospect a reason to peruse the catalog. In addition, teaser copy offers the opportunity to direct the prospect immediately to a particular page, spread, or to the order form.

Since envelope opening and catalog perusing are the first steps to response, any increase in this activity resulting from teaser copy should lift response. While not everyone who opens an envelope is going to respond, the more envelopes that are opened, the greater the chances of increasing response. Clearly, teaser copy is directly related to the strength of the offer. The stronger the offer, the stronger the teaser. But even without a powerful offer, effective teasers will add to envelope opening and catalog page turning more often than not.

The school market is generally one of limited mail dates, causing a large amount of promotion to reach prospects at about the same time. Particularly in the fall season, educators are likely to face mountains of mail. Those packages that get read must survive the initial selection process which includes envelope opening.

There are many educators who base their judgment to examine a mailing solely on the basis of the outer appearance of the promotion piece. Consequently, it is necessary to give educators a reason to open a promotion. Whether this reason is due to offer or product benefits, always use it to tease, tease, tease.

In addition to highlighting a point, corner cuts are useful ways to encourage a reader to turn a page. Including an arrow or the message "Details Inside" as part of a cut in the lower right-hand corner of a page can encourage the reader inside a catalog, self-mailer, or brochure.

Color Me Cheap

Just because a promotion is only 2-color doesn't mean it must be dull. Creative use of color can sometimes make a 2-color piece appear more colorful. Assuming a 2-color piece calls for black and a second color, it's possible to employ screens of both the color and the black (gray screen), reverse type in solid color or use solid type over solid color, screen an entire page to make it appear printed on colored stock, or use the second color to embellish illustrations. A word of caution, however: Do not get carried away with the second color. Judicious application is most effective.

Remember, four-color is not the only alternative to two-color printing. You can use 3-colors as well with great results. And by choosing certain shades you can mix color to achieve a multi-color look. For example, by using the process colors black, blue and yellow you can mix the blue and yellow for a green result. By varying the percentages of each color used in the mix, you can achieve a variety of tones.

One final note. Mailing on time is critical in the school market. Allow enough lead time so as to avoid rushing through the creative process. An unrealistic deadline almost always results in anxiety and stifled creativity. It can also increase the frequency of errors in the promotion.

As the complexity of the promotion increases, so does the amount of time necessary to create the piece. It isn't unusual to begin designing some promotions months ahead of their mail date in order to complete copywriting, photography, mechanical and film preparation, and printing on schedule. Most designers and copywriters will verify that the creative process can never begin too early!

CHAPTER 8

IMPROVING A DIRECT MARKETING CATALOG

THERE ARE THREE common mistakes most school marketers make when creating direct marketing catalogs. These errors include weak covers, insufficient merchandising, and difficult ordering instructions and policies. Improvement in these areas can have a major impact on better returns for one's direct marketing catalog dollars.

What Is A Catalog

A catalog should be a minimum of 16 pages. Anything with less pages does not exhibit response characteristics consistent with catalogs. Most are 8 1/2" x 11" although some are larger or smaller. One of the key physical characteristics of catalogs is their "heft." Catalogs distinguish themselves from other bulk mailings such as selfmailers or brochures through their additional weight and thickness.

Each catalog page should be designed to contain an optimum number of items per page, although this can vary greatly depending on the type

115

and number of items being promoted. But it's not as easy as dividing the number of products by the number of pages. For example, a 16-page catalog is planned to promote 100 different single disk supplemental software programs. Most pages will contain several programs but some pages should contain more than others. The best-selling programs should be featured on the beginning pages and allowed more space than poorer selling programs.

Although this is not usually recommended, it's even possible to create a catalog with only one item per page. Perhaps science kits, are being promoted, each of which contain 10-20 items for use in experiments. These kits may require an entire catalog page to fully describe each kit's purpose and benefits. However, it is not true that by allocating more space to an item that sales of that item will be automatically increased.

Catalogs are meant to be scanned and should be organized so items of interest to the scanner are easily recognized and understood. This leads to another important catalog characteristic.

Catalog copy should be terse. The reader should not have to search for descriptions or benefits. In some cases, one or two descriptive sentences per item are sufficient. If a product requires more, try including subheads and bullet statements to enhance the reader's ability to scan the material. Also be aware of type sizes. If a cover headline is in 34-point type, placing two paragraphs of 10-point type directly below the headline is not recommended. The reader's eye cannot easily adjust to the dramatic change in size, and chances are the two paragraphs will not be read.

Getting The Most From A Catalog

Organizing a catalog layout can sometimes be a monumental task. There is an analysis technique that can be applied when planning a catalog to ensure that the right amount of space and correct catalog position is allocated to the best selling, most profitable items.

The basic premise behind catalog layout strategy is that space in the catalog costs money. Consequently, space should be allocated in accordance with the ability of the item displayed to generate a profitable return. For example, if the best selling item generates ten percent of the total profit, it should receive a proportionate amount of sales space. It should also be positioned on a page in the catalog that provides the item the visibility it deserves.

The exceptions to this rule include front and back covers, order forms, and brand new items. Front and back covers are excepted because it is those areas that address the practical aspects of announcing the product line (front cover) and labeling the catalog for mailing (back cover). An order form should be provided whether or not it is returned with an order. And new items should be prominently introduced in order to generate continuing interest in the product offerings, though one can't be sure how well these new items will be received.

Another factor to be considered is categorizing or displaying items of a similar nature within a section of pages, much as a retail store has departments. Sometimes categories are formed on the basis of reader interest (grouping by grade level appeal for example), and sometimes they are based on product similarities (grouping by disciplines such as art, English, math, etc.). Grade level grouping often works best for elementary school products, while discipline grouping often works best for secondary school products.

Beginning With Analysis

Catalog layout planning begins with a mathematical analysis of the financial performance of the products to be included. Figure 11 is an example of such an analysis.

Figure 11

Catalog Product Financial Analysis

Category	Item	Cost of Goods/Item	Revenue/Item	Gross Profit Per Item
I	A	$12.00	$20.00	$8.00
	B	10.00	14.28	4.28
	C	8.00	13.33	5.33
	D	6.00	8.57	2.57
	E	4.00	5.00	1.00
	F	2.00	4.00	2.00
II	A	14.00	20.00	6.00
	B	12.00	20.00	8.00
	C	10.00	12.50	2.50
	D	8.00	13.33	5.33
	E	6.00	8.57	2.57
	F	4.00	8.00	4.00
III	A	10.00	16.67	6.67
	B	8.00	13.33	5.33
	C	6.00	8.57	2.57
	D	4.00	5.71	1.71
	E	2.00	5.00	3.00
	F	2.00	5.00	3.00

Categories I, II, and III could represent K-2 products (I), grade 3-4 products (II), and grade 5-6 products (III). Or these category groupings could represent Language Arts, grades seven to nine (I; Mathematics, grades seven to nine (II); and Science, grades seven to nine (III). Items A through F could be titles of books, software, videos, etc. Overhead is ignored in this example because it is presumed to be roughly equal for all products. If overhead differs from product to product, it should be provided for in the cost of the item.

Before Figure 11 can be converted into a catalog layout, the selling cost needs to be considered. In order to determine selling cost, the overall catalog cost must be allocated on the basis of space used to sell each product. This can be done in units of a page or in square inches of page space. In Figure 12, space has been allocated by units of a page.

Figure 12 is an example of what the space allocation for the items presented in Figure 11 might have been. The example assumes a sixteen-page, eight and one-half by eleven inch catalog where pages one, two, seven, eight, fifteen, and sixteen are reserved for cover, mailing area, order form, and new products respectively. Thus, the total space used in Figure 12 adds up to ten pages of the sixteen.

Let's assume the cost of the sixteen page catalog to be eight hundred dollars per thousand (including creative, printing and binding, list rental, mailing, and postage), and the mailing quantity is fifty thousand catalogs. Then the catalog per page cost is fifty thousand times eight hundred dollars per thousand divided by sixteen pages or $2,500 per page. Figure 12 further breaks this down into a promotion cost per item shown (one-half page costs $1,250 and so forth).

From Figure 11 we know the revenue and gross profit contribution per item. Figure 12 shows the promotion cost invested per item. From this

---

Figure 12

Catalog Space Allocation

Assumes a catalog per page cost of $2,500

Category	Item	Pages Allocated	Total Promotion Cost/Item
I	A	1	$2,500
	B	1/2	1,250
	C	1/2	1,250
	D	1/3	833
	E	1/2	1,250
	F	1/2	1,250
II	A	1	2,500
	B	1	2,500
	C	1/2	1,250
	D	1/2	1,250
	E	1/3	833
	F	1/2	1,250
III	A	1/2	1,250
	B	1/2	1,250
	C	1/3	833
	D	1/2	1,250
	E	1/2	1,250
	F	1/2	1,250

---

information, how many units each item must sell in order to pay for the cost of the space it occupies can be calculated.

Gross profit contribution means the difference between product cost and revenue for each item. The remaining gross profit contributes toward promotion cost, overhead, and pre-tax profit. By dividing the total promotion cost for an item by its gross profit contribution, one can calculate how many units must be sold in order to recover the promotion investment. If overhead is basically a fixed cost, then comparing gross profit contribution should give an accurate sense of the relative profitability of each item.

Calculating Break-Even Points

Figure 13 represents the calculated break-even point for each item in the sixteen-page catalog example.

By comparing the break-even requirements to the actual sales, oppor-

Figure 13

Catalog Product Financial Analysis

Category	Item	Contribution Per Item	Promotion Cost/Item	Sold Units Required To Break-Even
I	A	$8.00	$2.500	315
	B	4.28	1.250	292
	C	5.33	1,250	235
	D	2.57	833	324
	E	1.00	1.250	1,250
	F	2.00	1,250	625
II	A	6.00	2,500	417
	B	8.00	2,500	313
	C	2.50	1,250	500
	D	5.33	1,250	235
	E	2.57	833	324
	F	4.00	1,250	313
III	A	6.67	1,250	187
	B	5.33	1,250	235
	C	2.57	833	324
	D	1.71	1,250	731
	E	3.00	1,250	417
	F	3.00	1,250	417

tunities in the space allocation can be pinpointed. If actual sales data is unavailable because this is a first catalog effort, then sales for each item should be estimated and compared to the required break-even points.

For example, say the relationship between items A and B in Category I are as follows in Figure 14.

Figure 14					
Catalog Space Allocation Analysis					
Category	Item	Space Allocated	Units To Break-Even	Actual Units Sold	Dollars Profit
I	A	1 Page	315	140	($1,380)
	B	1/2 Page	292	400	$462

In the example in Figure 14, both items are from the same category and vie for respective space allocations within the total space allocated for the category. From Figure 12, it is known that item A takes up one page of space. Figure 13 shows that it contributes to gross promotion at the rate of $8.00 per unit sold. But in Figure 14, it does not even sell enough units to pay for its one page of space. Item B, however, using only one-half page, sold not only enough units to pay for its space, but enough to contribute $462 toward overhead and pre-tax profits. A reasonable action as a result of this analysis would be to trade space allocations between items A and B. In the next catalog, item A should be allocated one-half page and item B should be allocated one full page.

Allocating Space To Categories Of Items

As previously mentioned, when promoting through catalogs, it is advisable to categorize items in order to make it easier to locate product. Category space should be allocated first and then the per item space allocated within the category.

By summarizing the item and page data by category, comparison data can be developed. Summarizing from Figures 11, 12, and 13 and assuming sales data for each category results in the comparison shown in Figure 15.

Figure 15

Catalog Sales Comparison By Category

Category	Items	Total Promotion Cost	Average Gross Contr/Item To Promotion, Ovrhd/Profit	Catalog Pages	Assumed Actual Sales Units	Net Profit
I	6	8,333	$3.86	3 1/3	2,000	($613)
II	6	9,583	$4.73	3 5/6	2,500	$2,242
III	6	7,083	$3.71	2 5/6	3,000	$4,047

Based on the assumed sales performance in Figure 15, category I is generating the most profit. Category II, which is the second most profitable, receives the most space allocation. A re-allocation of space between Categories II and III would be in order. More space allocated to category III at the expense of both categories I and II would also be justified.

While this is not a simple analysis, it's also not terribly difficult, even for the smallest company where data must be hand gathered. It can be a very accurate tool for assessing the allocation of catalog space in a manner which provides the most opportunity to improve profits. Every catalog mailer should make the time to go through this exercise at least once each year.

Tips For The Most Important Pages Of A Catalog

Almost every promotion created has its own very unique aspects due to variables such as product, offer, audience, and promotion budget. Catalogs are no exception. However, there are some common aspects that apply to all catalogs such as pages that are consistently the most important in terms of generating reader interest and, consequently, product sales.

The most important pages of a catalog are those pages a prospect will see first. If these are of no interest, the prospect can't be expected to go searching any further through the catalog. The important pages are:

Front Cover
Back Cover
Front Inside Spread (pages 2 and 3)
Center Spread (in a stitched catalog)
Back Inside Spread (last two pages)
Order Form

The order of importance of these pages may vary depending upon what type of reader is receiving the catalog. Catalog readers fall into two general categories: Those who read front to back and those who read back to front. If a reader's attention has not been captured within a short period of time (10 to 15 seconds) with either the front or back sections of the catalog, chances are he or she will never venture inside.

The Front Cover

Reference catalogs (like some large textbook and school supply catalogs) can afford to have passive covers that do not attempt to call prospects to action. They can depend upon a school contract, a sales person, or some other relationship between the prospect and the catalog to cause involvement and readership.

Such is not the case with a direct marketing catalog. Only the words and graphics on the outer covers can create involvement with and readership of the catalog. Consequently, the outer covers serve one purpose alone — to command enough attention on the part of the reader to turn the cover.

There are three techniques available to school marketers to make their direct marketing covers compelling. These are strong benefit claims, intriguing offer copy, and competent graphics.

Benefit claims tell prospects what the product line will do for them. Strong benefit claims focus on the best features of the most popular products. Intriguing offer copy teases about the unique opportunities available to prospects. Compelling graphics make it impossible for prospects to miss these messages when scanning catalog covers as they pass through a stack of mail. The desired effect in combining these three elements is a catalog cover that one simply can't pass over.

Too often readership is presumed. It is presumed that because educational materials are being produced and/or distributed, an educator is somehow bound to consider and review the material. This is a dangerous presumption. Product lines will be better served if disinterest is presumed and compelling readership is the goal.

An interesting photo and corresponding headline will usually serve to accomplish the primary goal of the front cover. Chances are the scanner will look at the photo first and then glance at the headline. Give the photo some zip. Try and include people in the photo. A smiling teacher holding a workbook in front of eager, excited students will probably generate more interest than a shot of a spread of workbooks.

Another technique that can be applied is to promote reader identification. Try a headline such as *"Science Is Their Favorite Time Of Day Thanks To ACME Workbooks"* instead of simply *"ACME Science Workbooks."* After reading the first headline, there's a good chance the prospect will want to find out why these workbooks can make science exciting to students.

The inclusion of a good offer is another method that has proven to inspire readership. Developing a good offer is an art and it usually takes some trial and error to find a winner. The options are virtually unlimited and could be any one or combination of the following elements:

Discount	Free Trial
Guarantee	Free Product
Premium	

Another underutilized offer opportunity available to catalogers is the organization of sets of material at discounted prices. This process is also known as "bundling" and is often effective at raising the average order size for most catalogs. Select items that can be appropriately grouped together. Then package and promote them as a set at a discount in addition to offering them individually at full price.

Choose what is considered to be the most appealing offer and feature it on the cover in a headline, a burst, a banner, a corner cut, or as an inset. For example, assume a teacher's guide is free with every set of 30 classroom workbooks. The workbooks are also unconditionally guaranteed. One approach on the cover might be a headline of *"ACME Workbooks Are Guaranteed Forever"* along with a burst containing *"Free Teacher's Guide."*

The goal is to encourage the reader inside the catalog. Once a good offer has been created, don't make the mistake of telling the whole story on the cover. Tease about the offer to encourage the reader to turn the page and look inside for details. A popular method is placing a corner cut in the lower right hand corner with some teaser copy such as *"Free Gift - See Page 3."*

Finally, included somewhere on the cover should be the company name and address, the grade levels covered by the products in the catalog, and the season and/or year of the catalog. If space allows, also include any toll free telephone and/or FAX numbers.

The Back Cover

The back cover will probably include a mailing label area. Since this is the area containing the name or title of the recipient, there's a chance this may be the side first seen as a result of mail sorting. Therefore, the back cover could be the first side of the catalog viewed regardless of whether or not the prospect reads back to front. It pays to make the most of this page.

The post office requires that a catalog mailing area contains the indicia, return address, and room for a label. Meeting these requirements still leaves a large area. Here are some suggestions on how to better utilize space on the back cover.

Include any guarantee. Some coupon-type art surrounding the guarantee can help to highlight this benefit and make it look official.

Include any toll free numbers. Even if they are included on the front cover, it's perfectly acceptable to repeat them on the back where there may be more space to encourage their use. Many catalogs feature the toll free number on every page. A photo of an attractive phone representative with a phone to his/her ear is a great way to enhance a toll free number.

Additional suggestions would include repeating any special offers, highlighting a popular product, or featuring any free gift or premium. The company's goals or commitments along with an accompanying photo of a distinguished employee such as the president or editor-in-chief could also be included. This treatment is a nice way of highlighting a company's qualifications and establishing it's credibility within the industry.

Pages Two And Three

So often catalogs devote an entire inside front cover or page two to a letter from someone within the company organization. Keep this rule in mind. If the cover has stimulated enough curiosity for someone to turn the page, a letter from the president describing modern warehouse and office facilities on page two is probably not going to cement a sale.

Pages two and three are perfect places to sell. This area is where a company's most popular products should be featured along with any discounts, savings, or special offers. Also, while several products per page are the rule of thumb, it is perfectly acceptable to limit the products per page to three, two, or even one on the front inside spread.

Another important rule to remember is that when a page is turned from right to left, the reader's attention is usually focused on the right hand page since this page is revealed prior to the left page. That means page three is slightly more important than page two, page five takes precedence over page four, etc.

For example, let's imagine three popular software programs in science, math, and English are being promoted. Each sells for $29.95 but all three may be purchased for $59.95, a savings of almost $30. A suggestion would be to promote two of the programs separately on page two, promote the special savings of the set on the top of page three, and the last program separately on the bottom of page three.

The bottom of page three is also an excellent spot for any free gift or premium information. An exception to this rule would be in the case of a premium structure or choice of free item based on the quantity or amount purchased. The page prior to the order form would be a prime location for that type of premium offer. However, page three might be a nice place to hype the premium program in general with instructions as to which page features the actual premium items.

Last Two Pages

Remember those reverse readers? As with pages two and three, it is important to stimulate reader interest with the last two catalog pages, although a slightly different approach may be employed. Despite the fact that readers may begin at the back of a catalog, they usually realize that the information contained there may be different than the beginning of the catalog.

Rather than promoting the most popular products or repeating the information contained on pages two or three, it is perfectly acceptable to include products of lesser appeal. However, try to include product with special savings or advantages. A simple list of advantages may be included such as guarantee, toll free number, 30-day trial, shipment within two hours, etc.

If it is necessary to include an index in the catalog, the back pages are recommended. However, try to avoid the inside back cover and use this space more to an advantage.

The Order Form

Due to the heavy use of purchase orders in the school market, order forms usually serve to provide ordering information rather than as the actual ordering device. But this doesn't mean an order form can be taken for granted. Just because an order form is not actually returned doesn't mean it didn't play an important role in securing a purchase.

Unfortunately, many marketers find order forms rather boring. After all, creating a catalog cover can be much more fun and exciting. But the fact is, if the creative time and resources were allocated in proportion to the ability of each page in the catalog to contribute response, as much time and effort would be spent on the order form as on the cover.

Does the catalog order form pop out at potential customers or does it hide somewhere within the pages? Is it warm and friendly or is it foreboding and threatening? The answers to these questions could explain why sales are up . . . or down!

The decision to purchase has probably been made by the time a prospect gets to a catalog order form, but that decision is tenuous at best. If the customer can't decipher the order form, chances are the sale will be lost.

There are three basic qualities in a good catalog order form. First, the order form should be easy to locate. Second, it should be inviting in appearance. Third, it should be easy to understand. These are relatively easy qualities to effect, and they can have a good deal of influence on how well the catalog produces new business.

The Order Form Should Be Easy To Find

It is not uncommon for the direct mail browser to look for the order form in a catalog during the early stages of scanning. Generally speaking, the prospect expects to get a sense of how easy it is to buy the products presented within the catalog. The first step in this process is finding the order form. If the order form is hidden or missing, the browsing trip that may have turned into a shopping trip will probably come to an end.

There are a few steps catalog marketers can follow to make sure that a browser will always find the order form or, at the very least, information about how to order. One technique is to physically force the catalog to open at the order form. The simplest and least expensive method is to position the order form in the center spread. Other more expensive options include using a heavier stock for the order device or inserting a four page order form. Another option would be to insert a reply envelope or reply card at the order form position.

One could use the back cover as an order form. However, this is also relatively expensive because valuable selling space on the back cover must be sacrificed. In addition, there is the possibility that the whole catalog will be destroyed during the ordering process.

Another option is to announce the position of the order form in a burst on the cover, back cover, and throughout the text. This technique constantly gives the prospect instant access to the order form and eliminates interruptions to the momentum of the sale.

It's always a good idea to supplement the order form with information about what to do if the order form is missing. Some marketers prefer two order forms to cover impulse as well as later responses. Whether one or two order forms are included, the order form page should be reinforced with copy that says, *"Here's all you do to order if your order form is missing,"* along with instructions for ordering by mail or phone.

The Order Form Should Be Inviting

Unfortunately, many school marketers tend to create order forms that are more forbidding in their appearance than inviting. Many catalog order forms are covered with contract-size type stating a variety of requirements, terms and conditions. This can have a negative impact on a potential customer.

Educators who are new customers are going to be skeptical about the first business transaction. The appearance of the order form and the tone and manner of the "contract" copy is perceived as an indication of a company's attitudes. Educators, like all direct response consumers, don't want to take unnecessary risks with their direct mail purchases.

Design a simple order form — then make it simpler. Keep the information to an absolute minimum. Order forms where the information to be supplied is clearly numbered so prospects know they haven't missed anything is preferred.

Almost every catalog order form should carry an inviting headline such as, *"Here's All You Do To Order."* Some products are easier to order than others. It is recommended that the instructions include no more than three or four ordering concepts for quick, easy understanding by the prospect. It is not always possible to make the physical act of ordering simple, but it is possible to make the intellectual understanding of how to order easier than is often the case.

This concept of easy ordering can be extended visually as well. Number each step in the instruction copy and correspondingly number the area of the order form that it addresses. This gives the new prospect visual confirmation of the simplicity of ordering.

Take a look at the order form in Figure 16. At first glance, this ordering device gives the impression that it is relatively simple to understand and complete. Subheads like *"Easy Order Form," "Here's All You Do To Order," "Speed Your Order,"* and *"Choose Your Free Gift Here"* not only guide the customer through the order form, but they do it in a very positive manner.

The Order Form Should Be "Hassle-Free"

Since the school market is made up of mostly institutional buyers, include a *"ship to"* and *"bill to"* address on the order form. While the educator may be the individual to whom the product should be delivered, the bill will probably be paid by another position. Obtaining this information should expedite payment.

In addition, include a *"bill me"* option. There is little risk of bad debt as long as the shipment is sent to a school address. It does little to enhance an educator's career to practice theft from educational mar-

Figure 16

Easy Order Form

Here's All You Do!

1. Select the items you wish to order.
2. Complete the information listed below.
3. Mail or phone your order toll free. You may FAX your order or place it directly on our WEB site.

XYZ Education Company
209 School House Road
Smart City, CA 90909

Ship To:

Name _____

Title _____

School _____

Street _____

City _____

State _____ Zip _____

Telephone (____) _____
(This may expedite your order.)

Bill To: *(If different than shipping address.)*

Name _____

Title _____

School _____

Street _____

City _____

State _____ Zip _____

Telephone (____) _____

Means of Payment *(check one)*

☐ Check or money order enclosed.

☐ Bill me. *(Sorry, we can only extend billing privileges when billing to a school address.)*

☐ Bill school purchase order no.

☐ Charge to my credit card:
  ☐ VISA   ☐ MasterCard

_____
Card Number   Exp. Date

_____
Authorized Signature   Date

Enter Your Order Here:

Item Number	Description	Qty.	Price	Amount

			Subtotal	
			Add 10% Shipping	
			Total	

Speed Your Order
1-800-000-0000
8 a.m. to 5 p.m. weekdays
or FAX your order to 111-222-3333
or visit our website www.xyzedco.com

keters. The problem is much more likely to be the identification of duplicate orders due to purchase order confirmation. This problem can be controlled by requesting that all duplicate purchase orders be clearly marked *"confirmation"* and by asking order processing to check for duplicate conditions.

By the way, while almost all school marketers accept school purchase orders, too many incorrectly assume that this policy indicates credit is being extended. In fact, a school purchase order number is much closer to a hard cash transaction than it is to a credit offer which is more successful cash in consumer direct marketing by as much as 100%.

Make sure there's an area to indicate the premium if there's a choice involved. If shipping and handling charges have to be added include this information on the order form as opposed to a separate page and make it as simple as possible. Try to avoid shipping charges that require any type of calculation such as 25% of the subtotal. Include the company's name and address and a phone number whether or not it's toll free.

Don't clutter an order form with ominous paragraphs about unreasonable terms and conditions such as shipping damages, return authorizations, or missing merchandise. These restrictions only serve to imply to the prospect that it may be difficult to conduct business with the company.

Even though a particular business may require a minimum order size and/or written permission to return goods, these policies can be expressed in positive terms. For example, instead of *"Minimum Order Requirement,"* why not say *"Order ten or more and save on minimum order charge!"* Instead of *"Written permission is required in order to return merchandise,"* why not state, *"you may return anything you're unhappy with, but in order to assure proper credit to your account, please follow this procedure . . . "*

A powerful yet low cost marketing incentive is the guarantee. A guarantee or warranty is, at the very least, a positive statement about a company's faith in the quality of its products and, at the very most, a full money-back offer. The stronger the guarantee, the more possible it is to overcome resistance to order due to the prospect's unfamiliarity with a company.

A guarantee seems to have little effect on educators' attitudes toward a product once it's received, yet it seems to have a marked effect on their willingness to purchase. Interestingly, the educational bureaucracy contributes to the security of using powerful guarantees. In some cases, an educator would rather live with a purchase than go through the complicated business office procedures required to return the shipment. The simple fact is that educators don't order products with the idea that they will be returned. Educators order product because of their benefits. And, with few exceptions, unless the product is a tragic disappointment, educators keep it.

It's usually a good idea to publish a phone number on the order form and invite prospects to call if they need quick service or questions answered. FAX numbers and Web site addresses have also become popular. Regardless of whether or not the number is toll free, it's a good idea to let the marketplace know they are invited to communicate by phone. Aside from increasing response because some people prefer to call in their orders, printing a phone number will further assure new prospects that they are dealing with a reputable mail order company.

The Order Form Should Be User Friendly

Probably the most difficult aspect of a catalog is the actual ordering area. There are basically two approaches to order copy: 1) provide names and item codes and let the prospect fill in only quantity; 2) provide columns and headings and let the prospect fill in the name and description of each item as well.

Providing all the information is the preferred treatment when the number of items available is relatively small. However, presenting too much information can be as detrimental to response as presenting too little. When the number of items to be listed exceeds approximately twenty, this technique is not recommended. The information requires too much space and customers are presented with too many options before indicating their choice(s). The order form begins to take on the appearance of a tax form and becomes overbearing.

Major improvements can be brought about both in rate of response and average order size by adding intensity to a catalog cover, increasing the degree of merchandising, and simplifying ordering instructions and policies. These areas represent significant opportunities for those willing to take on the challenge.

CHAPTER 9

DESIGNING FLYERS AND SELFMAILERS

AT FIRST GLANCE, designing flyers and selfmailers may appear relatively easy when compared to a direct mail package or a catalog. After all, they are simply a single piece of paper that, when folded, is ready to mail. It is precisely the simplicity of this format that presents the challenge. While selfmailers and flyers can come in a variety of shapes and sizes, the fact is that all of the critical information that is found in larger formats must be included in these smaller promotions as well. This information includes:

	Mailing area (return address, indicia, label area)
	Product description
	Offer description
	Ordering information
Optional:	Order device
	Business reply copy (permit number, bar code, indicia, etc.)

What You Must Know

Keep in mind that prior to beginning the design process, several issues should be resolved. These include size specifications, number of colors and sides, product to be included, offer to be promoted, and the audience to be targeted. Once these issues have been decided, implementing a design is the next step in the creative process.

As an example, assume a selfmailer that is 11" x 17" and folds twice to become 5 1/2" x 8 1/2". Figure 17 illustrates how the selfmailer folds.

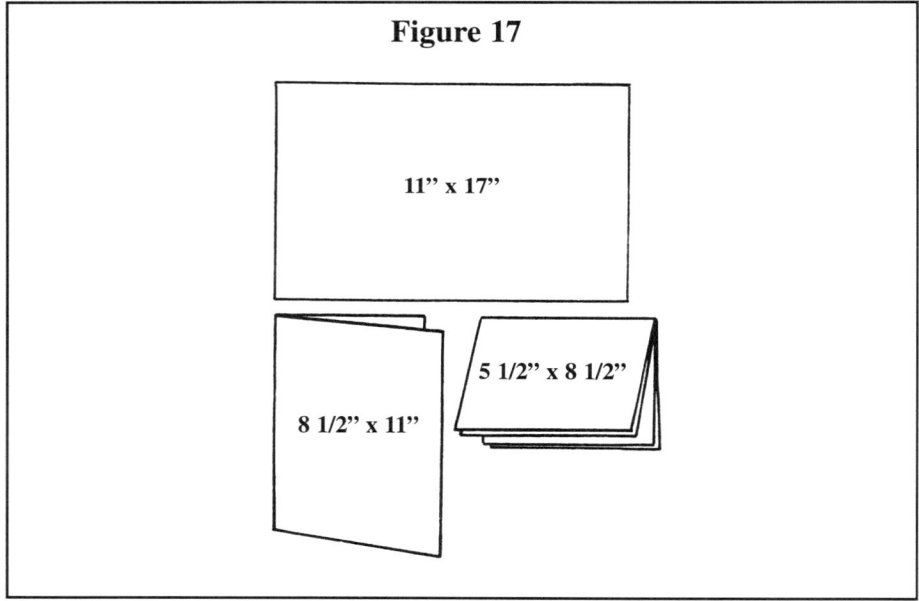

Figure 17

11" x 17"

8 1/2" x 11"

5 1/2" x 8 1/2"

The selfmailer is a two-sided, two-color piece. Three elementary reference books are being promoted that may be purchased separately or as a set at a 20% discount. This special offer expires August 31. The products are unconditionally guaranteed and the targeted audience includes librarians and classroom teachers in grades three to six.

Where To Begin

While certain information must appear in the piece, there are no hard and fast rules as to where it must appear. But there are certain areas of every selfmailer that are more visible than others and that are considered prime locations. These prime locations are where the most motivational information should be positioned such as the special savings and the fact the offer expires. Prime areas in this selfmailer example would include the front panels, back panels, and upper half of page 3 in that order.

It is helpful to begin the design process by creating a rough layout to allocate space for the basic elements that must be included in the selfmailer. Begin with those elements that are required and then move on to position optional information. Elements that are optional might include testimonials or information about the company. This rough design can be actual size or a scaled down version called a thumbnail sketch.

Since the format is a selfmailer, an area for the mailing label, return address, and outbound postage must be included. This information must appear on one of the two outside panels. In this example these elements will appear on the bottom half of the front cover.

A postage-paid order form is also included. When positioning this element, keep in mind that postal regulations prohibit the exposure of any business reply copy that appears on the reverse side of the order card. Therefore, the business reply copy will appear on the bottom of the back cover where, due to folding, it will be concealed during mailing. As a result, the order form copy will appear at the bottom of page three.

By starting with these two required elements that are limited to certain areas of the piece, the design process has begun relatively painlessly. The traumatic experience of putting pencil to paper (or fingers to keyboard) is over. The ice has been broken and feelings of relief begin to turn to confident excitement.

The two-page inside spread is where information on the three products along with details on the special discount available on the set will be presented. Since page three is considered prime space, let's position the set discount information on the top portion of page three above the order form followed by guarantee copy. That leaves page two to explain each of the three products.

The small area at the bottom of page three next to the order form would be a good location for a toll free number to speed ordering instead of mailing in the order form or in case it is missing. Conversely, a sense of urgency could be created by positioning copy regarding the expiration date of the offer next to the business reply card copy on the back cover.

The space remaining on the top portion of the front cover would be a good place to tease about the savings offered on the three book set. Since the mailing label is one of the first areas seen by the recipient, a sense of urgency can be reinforced by placing copy about the expiration date of the offer near the label.

Figure 18

In the space remaining on the back cover a suggestion might be a message about the company to promote credibility along with a photo of an appropriate representative such as the president or editor-in-chief. In addition, it would be a prime location for testimonials and guarantee copy.

Before you know it, the rough design is complete. All the elements necessary to the piece have been positioned. The actual design for this example is illustrated in the thumbnail sketches labeled Figure18. The next step is to execute the rough layout that has been created and decide how the selfmailer will actually appear.

The Chicken or the Egg

At this point a brief discussion of how copy and design are integrated is in order. It's really a question of which came first, the chicken or the egg.

While there are varied opinions on this subject, many prefer to complete a rough design prior to writing copy. It then becomes clear approximately how much space is available for headlines, subheads, copy blocks, and art elements. Of course, it is a rough design and space allocation can be adjusted as copy is developed.

For those who find designing a promotion to be much easier after copy is written, by all means continue with this method. Another approach would be to write copy after creating a rough layout but prior to a more comprehensive design. Whichever process is preferred, there must be give and take between copy and design as any promotion is developed.

Be Creative

As the rough is transformed into a more comprehensive design, creative options are limited only by budget constraints. Some creative suggestions would be the addition of product-in-use photos using real people for added interest. If art from the product is interesting, it can add a real flavor of the product to the piece. Consider showing actual pages of books, workbooks, or worksheets rather than just covers.

But don't feel as if every page must be filled with copy or art. White space used judiciously can encourage readability by removing the intimidation factor massive amounts of information can create. In addition, use heads and subheads to organize information and use short paragraphs instead of large copy blocks to make for easy scanning. Even though educators are the target, keep sentences simple and avoid technical or complex language.

Despite its restrictions, designing a selfmailer can be enjoyable. Determine the prime locations of the piece. Then position all the elements to be included, starting with those that are required and/or are limited to certain areas and continue with less motivational or optional information. Executing a design using this gradual approach can be far less intimidating and result in a more effective selfmailer.

Tips For Creating A Sale Flyer

Sale flyers can be one of the easiest direct mail pieces to create — or they can be the most difficult. A popular direct marketing notion is that a less sophisticated promotion piece conveys the biggest savings to the reader. Therefore, in its simplest form a sale flyer is a single sheet, printed in one or two colors. This design can resemble a newspaper insert and very effectively represent a discount theme with significant savings. However, there are some important creative concepts to keep in mind so that a sale flyer will have the best chances for success.

Promote A Sale Image

For maximum effectiveness, the fact that a flyer is promoting a sale should be prominently featured. Headlines and/or subheads should use words such as "sale," "discount," and/or "savings." Graphic enhancements can include such techniques as bursts, arrows, borders, and screens to highlight sale information.

Should a significant price savings be offered, the actual savings the customer will enjoy — and this is important — should be clearly designated. Too often this information is found only in the small print or not at all. For example, the headline may read *"Significant Savings On Software,"* but the pricing information reflects only the sale price per item, not the regular price or the savings incurred.

A common dilemma faced by marketers is whether to express savings as a percent or a dollar amount. First decide which approach will have more impact. While much depends on the value of the product being promoted, a rule of thumb would be not to mention any savings amount less than $5.00 or any discount less than 5%. Quite frankly, it is questionable whether a sale flyer is appropriate for discounts that are less than these amounts.

For example, software package A, which sells for $249.95 is offered at a discount of $20 or about 8%. A headline of *"SAVE $20"* would have more of an impact than *"SAVE 8%."* On the other hand, consider workbook A, which sells for $2.95 but is being offered for $2.39. In this case *"SAVE 20%"* packs more punch than *"SAVE 56 Cents."*

Keep The Product Description Simple

Product graphics can be simple line art or black and white photographs as long as they accurately portray the product. For example, line art should be appropriate to illustrate classroom desks and chairs. However, photography would probably be more appropriate for computer hardware. Keep in mind that if recipients of a sale flyer do not feel as if the product is clearly portrayed, they will be reluctant to order and response will be negatively effected.

Full-color can be used to enhance a product benefit. For example, the product on sale may be a book with beautiful four-color illustrations or a software program with interesting color graphics. If this is the case, consider the use of full- or four-color graphics. Although the four-color process may lend a more sophisticated and "upscale" look to a flyer and reduce the "sale" image, it is also important to accurately portray the product. A message of significant savings can be achieved through headlines, subheads, bursts, and other graphic techniques.

An offer can be enhanced with additional opportunities to save. For example, a sale flyer could consist of several items all offered at various savings. In addition, customers can enjoy a bonus discount depending on the total dollar amount of their order (i.e., $25 off on orders of $500+, $20 off on orders between $400 and $499, and so forth). And, any order received with a check might be eligible for an additional 4% savings. These multiple savings opportunities can create a virtual ordering frenzy!

There's nothing wrong with offering a free gift in a sale flyer. However, it should be combined with discounted pricing. After all, a sale flyer indicates that items are being offered at a savings. A free gift could be offered with orders over a certain amount or with sets of items.

Highlight Maximum Savings

Another sale flyer approach is to create sets of product and offer a discount on the set. For example, a series of classroom math workbooks for grades K through 6 could be discounted for each grade level as follows:

> 10 - 20 workbooks - 5% discount
> 21 - 30 workbooks - 10% discount
> 30+ workbooks   - 15% discount

Assume the regular price for each workbook is $1.95. A classroom set of 30 workbooks valued at $58.50 could be created for one grade level and offered at a discounted price of $49.95, a savings of $8.55 or almost 15%. In addition, a school building set of 30 workbooks for each of grades K through 6 could be created (210 books in all) for a $409.50 value and offered at a discounted price of $349.95 or a savings of almost $60 or almost 15%. The headline for a sale flyer promoting these sets should highlight the maximum savings available and might read something like *"SAVE UP TO $60!"*

Do not create a sale flyer made up entirely of slow moving product. Chances are that if these items have not sold well in the past, their performance will not be enhanced through a sale flyer. You may salt in a few "duds" at drastically reduced prices in an attempt to reduce inventory, but the majority of the promotion should contain product with sales appeal.

Following are the key points to keep in mind when creating a sale flyer:

1. Promote a sale image. Use simple promotion formats. Choose sizes, colors, and stock that allow proper product description while preserving a sale image.

2. Keep product description to a minimum.

3. Highlight maximum savings available and be sure and include specific information on exactly how the customer saves.

4. Keep graphics as simple as possible while portraying product accurately.

5. Offer as many opportunities to save as practical.

6. Do not create a sale flyer made up entirely of slow moving stock.

Sale flyers can be a relatively inexpensive method of generating additional revenue. Consider mailing a sale flyer to customers two or three times each year or more.

CHAPTER 10

PREPARING SPACE ADS THAT WORK!

PLANNING AND PREPARING a space ad is very much like baking a cake — proper ingredients must be combined correctly. In addition, the timing, frequency, and position of an ad are also important.

Unfortunately there is no single formula that produces the optimal space ad for all products. Average unit of sale, number of people involved in a buying decision, and buying season often dictate space strategy.

The broad applications of space include generating orders or leads, and informational advertisements. The choice between order-generating and lead-getting advertising should be a function of the level of difficulty in accomplishing a sale.

For example, if the average unit of sale is $30 or less, an order generating ad is probably the correct approach . Naturally, profit margin is a factor. But it is probably not cost effective to solicit and convert leads on a unit of sale this low. Even if the conversion is feasible, there is also a good chance of succeeding with an order-generating ad. The unit of sale is low enough that, most likely, there will be relatively few decision makers involved in the purchase.

On the other hand, an order-generating ad is probably not appropriate for high-ticket items. Odds are that the number of people involved in the decision to purchase is greater and an ad is a difficult media to accomplish a committee type of sale. Lead-getting followed by telephone, direct mail, or a sales call will probably prove to be a more successful approach.

Informational ads are those which make people aware of a new product or service or company position but do not solicit response. Though many of these ads will carry *"for further information write or call"* copy, it's clear from the design of the ad that the intent is to communicate a message, not solicit an inquiry.

Timing and frequency are also critical factors in advertising. Since most school buying decisions occur over several months in the spring, one-shot ads may not be as effective per ad as a series of ads might be. Products that require adoptions or previews probably should run with more frequency and start earlier than those that do not.

Employment of offer, copy, and art depend upon the type of ad that is planned. Lead-getting and order-generating ads are very similar but differ from informational ads. The main difference is the absence of offers and coupons in informational ads. This discussion will reference ads whose purpose is to generate leads or orders.

Rule Number 1: Always Use An Offer!

Offers are what put the direct in direct response. Offers provide the incentive to respond now, right this moment, and not sometime in the future. Of the three factors in producing a space ad — offer, copy, and art — the offer is the most volatile in affecting response rates.

Offers can take a variety of forms, but the most common are discounts, two for ones, buy one get one free, and premiums. Here are the headlines reflecting the offers used in some lead-getting and order-generating ads which have appeared in teacher magazines:

Take this $44.95 Language Development kit for $2.95!

Which one of these great activity packets would you like to have for only $1!

Special limited-time offer! Save $2.00 each!

Wow! Save money on inexpensive classroom rewards.

Free: 2 new books with your subscription!

There is a natural inclination to approach the planning of an ad from a product point of view, focusing on product benefits. But it is a mistake to use a space ad to attempt to convert a non-user to a user with product benefits. As the readers of any publication, users of your product type will contribute the overwhelming portion of response, as they do in almost every media. The only exception would be brand new products or services.

A better approach when planning lead-getting or order-generating ads is to ask two questions. First, how can the scanner be enticed to read the ad and second, how can the user be prompted to respond? A good solid offer will do more to help accomplish these goals than any other aspect of the ad.

Developing Offers

While the variety of offers is virtually limitless, they all fall into one of two types:

Credit offers: Send no money! Simply mail in the handy order device and we'll send a bill along with your widget.

Cash with order offers: Just send your check or money order to this address, and we'll ship your widget right away!

Generally speaking, given no other variables, a credit offer will respond better than a cash offer by as much as two to one. However, it does not automatically follow that a credit offer should always be used. The choice between the two should be decided on the basis of the media or lists that are being targeted, and the economics of the particular situation.

For example, credit offers may be used when promoting to customers. Customers are proven buyers and the risk of high returns or bad debts should be directly related to the perceived value of the offer. If the product being promoted is of the same quality customers have experienced and the price does not exceed other comparable products, the increase in sales brought about by using a credit offer should far outweigh the return or bad debt factor.

A space ad usually reaches a broad range of people and it is often impossible to control audience selection. While credit offers are not the most risk-free offers to use in this medium, they do offer certain benefits. Credit offers have a way of dispelling prospects' concerns that they may be taken advantage of. Credit offers are also the easiest types to which prospects can respond as they eliminate the preparation of checks or requests for purchase orders.

For those marketers who have never promoted through space advertising, consider a cash with order offer or purchase order number requirement for lower units of sale, and a lead-getting approach for higher units of sale. When conducting a credit test, be sure to qualify each order through one or more of these techniques:

1. Ask for a school name and address
2. Ask for a signature
3. Ask for a telephone number

Rule Number 2: Always Back Products With A Guarantee

Guarantees help to pacify a prospect's concern regarding a company's reliability. Guarantees can be money-back when the product is returned, money-back when the product is returned in a reusable con-

dition, and full credit as opposed to full refund. The main point is that
none of these guarantees should have any detrimental effect.

Teachers are usually good credit risks, especially if the name and
address of their school is required. But often magazines — even
teacher magazines — have other readers as well. Until it is experienced, one cannot be certain of the credit quality of a readership.

In the school market, a school purchase order number is usually as
good as cash, though it may add 60 to 120 days to the receivable. A
purchase order number should be an option to cash with order in most
instances.

Naturally, an important part of employing an offer is in its presentation.
This leads to a discussion regarding space advertising copy and art.

Rule Number 3:   Assume No One Wants To Read A Space Ad

Most people don't like to read so they often need motivation. Since
most people scan, the copy and art in a good space ad should accommodate this scanning process.

When planning copy and layout, the first concern should be impact
while the second concern should be communication. Here's a set of
ground rules for planning space ad copy and design:

• The eye of the reader must be caught within 10 seconds.

- At best, "visual images" used to draw the prospect into the ad are limited to two (a photo and headline or a headline and subhead).

- If the prospect is drawn into the ad, the third item read is probably the coupon or contract copy.

Communicating through a space ad is not at all like communicating through a personal letter. Readers will accommodate personal letters but not space advertisements. An ad must be developed to accommodate the reader.

Catching "The Eye" Of The Reader

The two elements that will capture attention are headlines and visuals. Visuals tend to be more appropriate for larger-sized ads because they have a much better opportunity to achieve impact. Headlines can be effective in large or small ads, but they must be well written, catchy heads.

The coupon (when there is one) is where a direct response buyer looks to get a "capsule report" of the offer. Avoid coupons that are difficult to understand or incomplete. Ask for as much information as is needed to qualify and execute the sale (or lead follow-up) and no more.

It's also a good practice to keep the ordering options to as few as possible. Generally, the more decisions required of the prospect, the less response will be received.

Body copy is usually the last information a prospect digests. By this point, the prospect is usually interested so the body copy should be heavily slanted toward pointing out benefits to the buyer. Since the buyer is the individual that is encouraged to respond, if room allows, highlight benefits to the user.

The Purpose Of Art And Design

Designing a space ad should be as different from creating an illustration as is auto repair. The whole purpose of design and art for a space ad is to stop the roving eye of the reader and communicate the proposal (offer) as quickly and clearly as possible. Ads that have a balanced look may not be as effective as those that are "unbalanced."

Keep in mind that there is a dual purpose to design: To command attention and to communicate about the product or service. Many ads achieve one objective or the other, but few ads accomplish both. Consider the space ad with so much copy crammed onto a page that the idea of reading it is distasteful because it appears to be too much work. On the other hand, many ads using catchy headlines or photos stop the scanner only momentarily, allowing the reader to continue on through the periodical without the first idea of the product or service that was promoted.

As mentioned, planning and preparing a space ad can be compared to baking a cake. Unfortunately, there are no space ad cookbooks available so marketers have to make and test their own recipes. As advertising efforts are developed and refined, use these guidelines to avoid disasters:

- If a winner is developed — stick with it.

- If coupon-style ads are run believing that they help school purchase order business but no appreciable coupon response is received, an informational ad format may be a better choice. The coupon takes up valuable space.

- If a space ad is not contributing to purchase order business nor generating any appreciable response, stop the ad. Try another approach, use another media, or run the ad at a different time. Running space ads simply because the competition uses space is not sufficient reason to employ a format that does not produce.

- Timing and frequency are as integral to space ad results as they are to those from other forms of direct mail. Ads aimed at school funded purchases usually require sustained exposure over the buying decision period. Ads aimed at teacher funds need not be sustained yet the issue date may be critical. Decide the nature of the space ad and plan its release date(s) as one would with any direct mail effort.

CHAPTER 11

TELEMARKETING: COULD IT WORK FOR YOU?

TELEMARKETING HAS A limited application in the school market. It isn't for everyone or for everything. When the circumstances are right it is an extremely powerful medium that has the ability to increase sales almost "at will." When those circumstances are wrong, it can be utterly disastrous.

There are some very definite advantages to telemarketing over other forms of direct response promotion. Consider the following positive aspects:

Tracking Is Easy

Most school marketers know how frustrating tracking promotion results can be. Most school purchase orders offer few clues regarding from which list or, in some cases, from which promotion effort an order is the result.

In many ways, telemarketing is easier to monitor than any other form of marketing. Tracking is almost 100%. Not only is it possible to determine which campaign produced the response, it is possible to know exactly from which school the order came, the name of the person ordering, and his or her position in the school.

Unlike other forms of mailed campaigns, response is immediate. As soon as the call is completed, such data as whether or not an order has been received, the dollar amount of the order, which product has been requested, and the quantity ordered is known. The 10- to 14-day waiting period between mail date and first response is eliminated.

Better Promotion Budget Control

Within reason, telemarketing can be "turned on" and "turned off." For example, if a sales budget in the last quarter of the year is running behind, turn on some telemarketing and bring it back on target. Conversely, because response is immediate and it is possible to monitor a telemarketing campaign on a daily basis, actual calling can be terminated at any time.

Unlike a mailed promotion effort, it is possible to determine if a phone campaign is unprofitable before spending the entire promotion budget allocated to the program. If the telemarketing results are not acceptable, liabilities can be limited by simply turning off the effort and owing only for the hours called to that point.

If it is difficult to determine why sales are disappointing, simply ask the callee why they aren't buying. Telemarketing is one of the few sales media that allows one to sell and gather marketing information in the same effort.

Revise A Campaign In Progress

Another positive feature of telemarketing is its flexibility. If an aspect of the campaign doesn't seem to be working, it can be changed. For example, suppose many of the prospects reached respond that they would love receiving the product but the price is too high. Simply alter the price, if possible, and continue calling.

Eliminate Some Of The Guesswork

This brings up another advantage to telemarketing. The direct, immediate, and individual feedback makes it possible to gain a much better idea of why particular results have been obtained and whether or not they indicate success. Valuable information such as whether or not the premium was motivational, the price was too high, a demand for the product exists, or the northeast is more productive than the southwest is immediately available.

It's also an ideal opportunity to obtain some limited information about a product or company. Ask prospects if they would be interested in receiving information about a new product being considered to determine if there is a market. When calling customers, ask them why they have purchased in the past. These questions, however, should be kept to an absolute minimum (one or two) and it is helpful if the question is presented with multiple choice responses.

Telemarketing Isn't For Everybody

While telemarketing may appear to be the ideal form of direct response marketing for the school market, it does have its disadvantages. Before abandoning all other forms of promotional efforts in favor of the exclusive use of telemarketing, here are some issues to consider.

The availability of the individual that must be reached by phone is critical. For example, classroom teachers and department chair people usually do not have easy access to a phone nor schedules that allow them to accept random calls. Reaching them by phone is not usually cost effective. Although most school personnel will return calls, particularly if left an 800 number, this causes a number of administrative problems for telemarketers. The best controls seem to be administered by outbound calling.

On the other hand, district personnel, principals, librarians, or school secretaries are good prospects for phone solicitation. In addition to having access to a telephone, most of these contacts are also likely to have access to a budget and the ability, within reason, to make decisions about spending that budget. This is seldom the case with classroom teachers.

Consequently, as a general rule, it's best to avoid products requiring committee decisions to purchase such as expensive computer equipment. It is not cost effective to reach someone who seems interested in a product and offer only to find out that the decision to purchase lies with a group of twelve individuals.

As with other forms of direct response marketing, it is important to attempt to match the product with the individual most likely to respond. If the purchase decision for the product will not be made by someone within the school that is cost-effectively available by phone, chances are telemarketing is not appropriate. For example, it is probably not beneficial to call a school secretary about a product only a classroom teacher would consider simply because the secretary is easier to reach by phone.

Telemarketing Isn't For all Product Lines

Marketing by phone has limitations when it comes to describing products. Unlike a mailed piece, the opportunity to describe a product through photos, illustrations, or long blocks of copy does not exist. A verbal explanation of the product and offer is the only means of description on which to rely.

Consider the full color computer software program that operates by voice commands and can be used by a classroom of 30 students simultaneously. It probably could not be easily described over the phone. However, the phone may be an appropriate way to generate sales leads for an in-school demonstration. Likewise, if marketing 7,000 items in a 500-page catalog, telemarketing is not recommended. However, within the catalog there is probably a product or set of products that could be effectively sold by phone.

Remember to keep the call brief. No one wants to listen to 10 minutes of uninterrupted product or offer description nor would the callee retain what had been said. Description of the product and offer should be limited to a 2 to 3 minute phone conversation. The goal, of course, is to maximize the number of contacts for the best sales results. The longer it takes to describe an offer and/or product, the less calls can be made per hour.

Any product chosen for telemarketing should be one of the more popular rather than a poor seller. Chances are that if it hasn't done well through other media it will do no better through telemarketing.

Beware Of Bad Debt And Returns

The decision to purchase as a result of telemarketing is often arrived at differently than other forms of advertising. For example, some people are not comfortable saying "no" to the friendly voice on the other end of the phone. They may wish to end the call quickly and simply say "yes" without understanding to what they have agreed. They may completely misunderstand the product and/or the offer. And, because they have nothing to remind them of their decision once the call is terminated, they may forget the commitment entirely.

Consequently, returns and/or bad debt can be substantially higher when telemarketing. However, the risks involved can be reduced by shipping promptly, issuing letters or postcards confirming orders quickly, or both. In addition, a rule of thumb to use when telemarketing is that sending a mailed piece to prospects prior to contacting them by phone can increase the success of a telemarketing program from 3 to 5 times.

Organizing The Offer

As with any other type of promotion, it is important to include a strong offer or incentive to purchase in addition to the product's educational benefits. This could take the form of a special discount, a premium, buy four and get one free, etc. Options in this area are really limited only by one's ability to describe the offer so it's easily understood over the phone.

Guarantees, previews, and/or trials are especially important when tele-marketing. Potential customers want the assurance that they can review and return anything to which they agree to accept by phone with no obligation. Remember, prospects must rely solely on a verbal description of the product and their interpretation of that description may be completely unlike what was intended. They also have a tendency to forget their commitment when they hang up the phone. If prospects feel there is no recourse should the product be different than the way it was perceived, they'll probably say "no."

Offering a trial examination is recommended and often is the only way to telemarket. It can be very difficult to get a hard order on the telephone because of the involvement of purchase orders. In most cases, a trial order can be accepted without issuing a purchase order but a hard order cannot. This process of receiving a purchase order number is enough to cripple a telemarketing campaign. As it is, a number of schools will follow the receipt of the trial order with a purchase order. This often results in some percentage of duplicate shipments because the telemarketer is unable to match up the trial order with the purchase order.

Response can be enhanced by extending the offer beyond a trial order to include a discount. There has been some limited success with premium offers, but the discount seems to be considerably more successful on the telephone.

Price is an important consideration when marketing by phone. Due to the cost per hour of phoning and the number of contacts per hour, not all products are priced for profitable telemarketing. Consider creating a set or group of related products to offer by phone. As with other medium, there's nothing wrong with creating a special offer strictly for telemarketing — in fact, it's preferable.

Customers vs Prospects

The difference in success between a telemarketing campaign to a customer or customer school vs a prospect or prospect school can be dramatic. Interestingly, the "front-end" or number of trials ordered per hour can be remarkably similar. The difference is often concentrated in the "back-end" where the pay up and return rates can combine for some startling differences.

Customers are more receptive to calls from companies they recognize and are more likely to be predisposed toward that company's products. Often prospects do not seem to remember the telephone call or, at least, the details of the offer. And a number of them take the position that the trial shipment is unsolicited merchandise.

Calling customers and offering them a special deal available only to them is one recommendation. Remember, this group has purchased from you before and, therefore, will generally be more receptive to your call. It is a good idea to maintain a customer file that includes phone numbers whether or not telemarketing is a current consideration.

A Note About Billing And Shipping

Both the timeliness and the wording of the billing and shipping terms can have a significant impact on the conversion of trial orders to net sales. The faster the shipment, the higher the conversion to sales while the slower the shipment, the lower the conversion to sales. By the same token, the more directly the invoice refers to a trial order by telephone the higher the conversion to sale. The less that reference is made, the lower the conversion to sales.

One technique that can be used to enhance conversion to sales is to issue a confirming letter or postcard immediately upon making a trial sale. Those can be issued by the telemarketing personnel themselves, bypassing normal fulfillment procedures and their typical lead times. It can only help conversion rates to remind educators they agreed to a trial examination on the phone.

Similarly, one must be careful when calling in late Spring. If a trial shipment should arrive after school is out, the resulting conversions to sales will almost certainly be disappointing.

Developing A Telemarketing Script

Regardless of the product or prospect, following are a few rules of thumb to remember when developing a phone script:

Immediately identify the caller. The opening of almost every tele-marketing script should be something like, "Hello, this is (caller's name) calling for (the name of the company promoting the product or service)." Since the call is probably unsolicited, any confusion on the part of the prospect should be eliminated early in the call. Giving the caller's name and company with which he or she is associated should avoid any misunderstanding regarding the nature of the call.

Keep the script simple. Make sentences short, avoid complex words or terms, and use minimal product description. While the script should include all pertinent information, for the sake of economy the length of each call should be kept to a minimum. If prospects have specific questions, they will ask for further explanation.

When telemarketing, one must rely on a verbal rather than written description of the product and offer. Prospects often do not have written material that they can read and reread for complete understanding. Long, involved product or offer descriptions will not be easily understood over the phone and can discourage ordering.

Solicit responses from the prospect. Droning on for five or ten minutes describing a product and offer is not likely to stimulate interest on the part of the prospect. Chances are they will become bored and look for a way to terminate the call. Therefore, it is advisable to salt in a few simple questions directed at the prospect throughout the call to help involve the prospect in the conversation.

For example, after the caller identifies him/herself and the company they may ask, "How are you today?" If a mailed piece was sent to the prospect prior to the call one may ask, "Do you have the literature we sent you in the mail handy, Mrs. Smith?" After describing a product benefit follow up with, "Don't you think that Rainbow bulletin boards would brighten the classrooms in your building, Mr. Brown?"

These techniques will help to make the call less of a sales pitch and more of a friendly chat. It should also encourage the prospect's attentiveness and reduce the tendency to become distracted. However, don't get carried away and expect the prospect to respond after every other sentence. Two or three questions of this type are probably plenty in any average phone script.

Also, the answers to any questions should not effect the flow of the call. The questions should be of a nature that, regardless of the answer received, the caller can continue with the script. For example, if the literature sent to the prospect by mail is not handy, simply assure the prospect that's OK, they don't have to search for it, and continue on.

Prepare more than one closing. When the point in the call is reached asking for a commitment on the part of the prospect, be prepared for both a "yes" and "no" answer. If the answer is "no," try to encourage the prospect to reconsider.

Some approaches to negative responses might be to remind the prospect that there is no risk, the product is guaranteed, they can receive a full refund at any time and/or they can review the product at no charge for 30 days. Another approach might be to reduce the commitment by asking if the prospect would like to accept a portion of the product rather than the original offer (i.e., choose individual books rather than the full set of 25 volumes).

If the answer is still "no," it is usually advisable to terminate the call rather than continuing to a point that might become annoying to the prospect. That would only serve to promote a bad reputation for your company. An appropriate closing might be, "Thank you for your time. I'm sorry I couldn't help you today."

On the other hand, if the prospect accepts the offer it is advisable to confirm the terms and conditions of the offer and the shipping information (address, name, etc.). It is also advisable to ask if there is a separate billing address and to take that information as well. Of course, make sure to thank them for their order.

Be flexible. The script is meant to act as a guide for the caller and is not, by any means, cast in cement. For example, if the prospect shows no interest in how much he can save but rather in what colors the product is available, by all means encourage callers to respond to the prospect's interests. Keep in mind that one of the advantages of telemarketing is the one-on-one contact with the prospect which allows the ability to tailor the promotion approach specifically to that individual.

It's also acceptable if each caller uses language with which he/she is comfortable rather than reading the script verbatim as long as the original meaning is not misconstrued. Once experienced callers have become familiar with an approach and product, it is not uncommon for them to very rarely even refer to the script.

As previously mentioned, as an option it is possible to conduct a mini survey while telemarketing. For example, if customers are being contacted one may ask why they have purchased from a particular company in the past. This can indicate which benefits or policies are important to customers (i.e., speedy shipping, guarantees, good quality, low prices, etc.) so that they may be promoted more strongly in the future.

Any survey questions should be asked just prior to closing the conversation. They should also be limited to only one or two questions. If the answer to the question cannot be stated simply as "yes" or "no," offer a selection of specific answers from which the prospect can choose. For example, asking why a customer has purchased in the past, follow up with "was it because of good service, low pricing, or our guarantee policy?" This approach will help to categorize answers so that results will be statistically significant.

Prepare a fact sheet and attach it to the telemarketing script. The fact sheet will provide an easy reference of important information for the caller. It should include items such as price, number of weeks until the product will be received, a complete product description, guarantee, pertinent company policies, and any other information that may be important to the program. If asked a question, the caller can refer to their fact sheet rather than wading through the body of the script for the answer. Also, it is not practical to include all the information usually found on a fact sheet in the body of the script.

Choose callers carefully. Not everyone is cut out to be a telemarketing representative. There are certain qualities a good caller should have such as an appealing phone voice, good diction, a pleasant manner, and the ability to improvise easily and intelligently.

Perhaps the most difficult aspect of telemarketing is the ability to overcome the constant rejection. Callers can experience hang-ups and verbal abuse as well as busy signals, no answer, and no orders. It takes a special kind of person to overcome these negatives and still remain pleasant and unruffled. If an experienced in-house telephone staff is not available, engaging an experienced telemarketing company to make your calls is strongly recommended. The chances for success can be greatly improved.

Monitoring A Telemarketing Campaign

Don't despair if the first day of calling ends with disappointing results — even the most seasoned callers take a while to become familiar with a product and comfortable with the script. One can usually expect a significant improvement during each day of the first week or two of calling. This assumes the calls are made by the same people and the days of calling are consecutive.

If there is no previous telemarketing experience to which to compare results, it is recommended that a program be continued at least two to three weeks before it is discontinued. Otherwise the results will be statistically insignificant and any conclusions drawn will not be valid.

Once again, remember that the program can be altered at any time while it is in progress. It's important to monitor a program closely in its early stages in order to work the "bugs" out. Interacting with the callers periodically throughout the program is important, but is especially so during the initial stages.

Listen to the callers as they make their contacts. If they are not reacting as anticipated, make suggestions for improvement. All callers do not necessarily feel comfortable with all programs.

It's impossible to predict every possible situation. Callers are probably going to run into situations about which they will have questions during the first few days of the program. Meet with them periodically through the start-up and be available throughout the program to offer solutions to any problems they raise. If callers do not know the answer to a prospect's question, recommend that they admit they don't have the information but will find out and call back rather than fabricate an answer.

Pay attention to prospects' reactions — both positive and negative. If 60 percent of the "no's" reject an offer because the price is too high, maybe a price reduction should be considered. If prospects are not readily available late in the afternoon, perhaps calling should be limited to earlier in the day. If prospects seem interested in a benefit not mentioned in the script, perhaps it should be added.

Suppose the "worst case" has occurred and the telemarketing attempt has been rejected as unprofitable. The feedback from those people contacted can be invaluable when developing product, offer, policies, etc. Telemarketing is one of the very few promotion techniques where it is possible to actually find out why no orders were generated.

What To Do When An Order Is Received

Once a successful call has been completed, there is the danger that the prospect may forget the terms to which he/she has agreed. While it is always important that product be shipped promptly, it is particularly important when telemarketing. It is advisable that a letter be included in each shipment explaining that the package is the result of a telephone sale. The letter should then restate the terms and conditions of the sale. The goal is to avoid any confusion over "unsolicited merchandise."

Unless it is possible to ship product within 24 hours of a telemarketing sale, it is also recommended that an acknowledgment card be sent immediately after the call, prior to the shipment of the product. The card could take the form of a simple, preprinted 3" x 5" postcard with optional fill-in spaces for name, product, price, etc. that the caller can easily complete after ending a successful call. This card will serve to quickly remind prospects in writing of their phone commitment and that they will be receiving product soon.

How To Analyze A Telemarketing Effort

To anyone familiar with analyzing the results of direct mail programs, telemarketing poses a unique challenge. Whereas direct mail lends itself to analysis in total, telemarketing is better examined as a rate of success.

In direct mail, there is no escaping the total investment. One mails 100 thousand pieces and bears the total cost of that endeavor. Incoming orders are accrued against that initial investment and, hopefully, provide an acceptable rate of return.

In telemarketing, there is also an initial investment, but it is far from the total cost of the campaign. It is mostly in the form of script preparation, list preparation, telephone look ups, and training. Once calling begins, telemarketing becomes an hourly investment.

How does one make the evaluation of whether or not a telemarketing program is a success? Conversion of all the relevant factors to hourly rates helps. Essentially, profitability is calculated by the hour.

Therefore, in addition to the statistics usually gathered during other forms of direct response marketing, there are some additional items that should be monitored when telemarketing for a complete analysis. Following is a list of the basic information recommended be maintained for each day of calling:

- Total hours called
- Total cost of hours called
- Cost per hour of calling (total cost for hours called divided by total hours called)
- Total number of sales
- Number of sales per each hour of calling
- Total revenue
- Total revenue per hour of calling
- Number of refusals
- Number of completed calls

- Number of completed calls per hour
- Number of leads used
- Sales as a percentage of completed calls (sales divided by completed calls)
- Sales as a percentage of total leads (sales divided by total leads used)

Figure 19 shows the factors necessary to analyze a typical telemarketing campaign. Note that these factors have been converted to hourly rates.

Figure 19

Hourly Revenues and Expenses For Hypothetical Telemarketing Campaign

Gross Revenue	$ 237
Projected Returns	78
Net Revenue	159
Cost of Goods	43
Contribution to Promotion, Overhead and Profit	116
Telemarketing Expense	50
Contribution to Overhead and Profit	66
% Return on Investment Before Overhead	71%

Of course, the ultimate measure of success will be the total revenue minus total costs or net profit. However, the additional information previously listed can help determine why a program has succeeded or failed. For example, if revenue is below expectations it would be helpful to determine if that was due to a low rate of contact or because of a high number of refusals. A poor contact rate could indicate the need for improvement in list selection, that the availability of the contact is poor, or that the time of day calls are being made should be altered. Refusals, on the other hand, could indicate the price is too high, there is no demand for the product, or the product or offer cannot be easily understood by phone.

A few additional comments about the hourly characteristics of telemarketing are in order. The projectability of results are effected by the sample size on which they are measured. Therefore, one needs to accumulate somewhere between 100 and 200 hours of calling in order to have a reliable base from which to project.

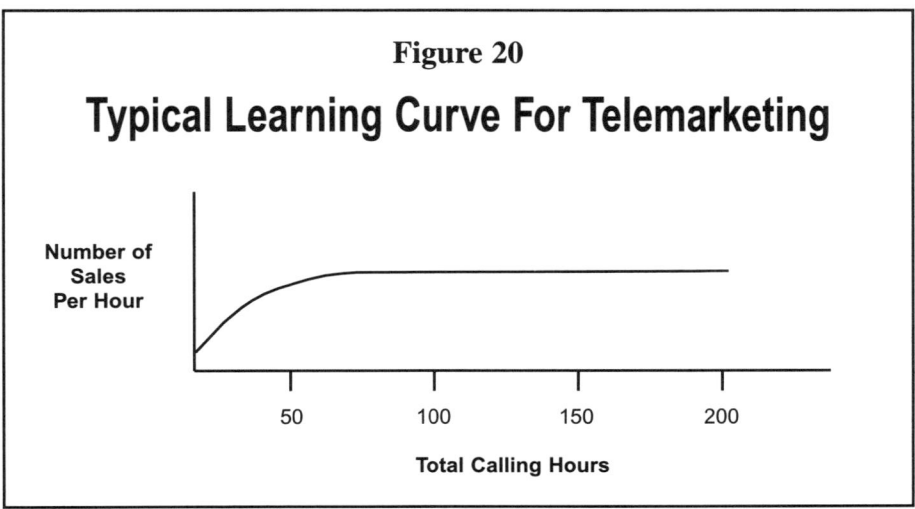

Figure 20

Typical Learning Curve For Telemarketing

The early hours of any telemarketing program represent a learning curve that is represented in Figure 20.

It is not uncommon to see dramatic increases in sales per hour, especially during the first 100 hours. When possible, a good way to evaluate a start-up is to run a test for 200 hours and then analyze the total effort and the last 100 hours separately shown in Figure 21. This will

Figure 21

Hypothetical Telemarketing Analysis
Start-Up vs Additional Hours

	Per Hour Results		
	Average	1st 100 Hours	2nd 100 Hours
Gross Revenue	$ 237	$ 120	$ 354
Projected Returns	78	40	117
Net Revenue	159	80	237
Cost of Goods	43	22	64
Contribution to Promotion, Overhead and Profit	116	58	173
Telemarketing Expense	50	50	50
Contribution to Overhead and Profit	66	8	123
% Return on Investment Before Overhead	71%	11%	108%

Errata

On page 123, **Allocating Space to Categories Of Items**, there was an error made in paragraph 3. The paragraph should read:

Based on the assumed sales performance in Figure 15, category III is generating the most profit. Category II, which is the second most profitable, receives the most space allocation. A re-allocation of space between Categories II and III would be in order. More space allocated to category III at the expense of both categories I and II would also be justified.

help to separate the start-up from a more representative sample of the program.

Still Wondering If Telemarketing Is Appropriate?

Consider telemarketing when these conditions converge:

1. The promotion can be made to a customer or to a customer's school.
2. The callee can be brought to the phone with reasonable cost effectiveness.
3. The product or service can be made available for a trial examination period.

If it is still not clear whether or not phone solicitation is a suitable form of marketing for your situation, consider testing a telemarketing effort. Because it can be more readily controlled than other forms of marketing, testing this medium can be relatively inexpensive. Basic costs to conduct a phone test would include the list cost, cost per hour of phoning, and script development. Other enhancements might include a direct mail piece sent to the prospect prior to the call and/or a post card sent to confirm each order. If phone numbers are not provided with the list, there would also be a charge to manually look up each number.

Given the right circumstances as described in this chapter, telemarketing can offer significant opportunities to school marketers. However, as with other forms of direct response marketing, telemarketing should be carefully planned and executed for the best results.

CHAPTER 12

HOW TO IMPROVE THE EFFICIENCY OF A SALES FORCE

MANY COMPANIES IN the education market employ a sales force to market their products and/or services. There's nothing like that one-on-one, personal approach when trying to cement a sale. And if the cost of the product or service is significant, a sales force can be a necessity.

A sales force can offer a number of advantages not available through other marketing approaches:

- Immediate response to questions or concerns regarding the product and/or service.
- The flexibility to identify with and appeal to a variety of individuals and job functions.
- Product demonstrations and one-on-one sample distribution.
- User training sessions.
- A feeling of buyer security resulting from actually meeting the person behind the product and/or service.

In fact, when it comes to influencing orders, a sales force often can offer the best potential for results. But, as with all good things, there is a down side. In the case of sales forces, the bad news is that their costs can be high and their rate of efficiency can be low.

For example, a direct mail package has the potential to reach the entire teacher market universe in one mailing. It could take a sales staff of 100 people years to cover the entire universe of teachers. Cost per order for a profitable direct mail campaign could be as low as under $10. On the other hand, costs per order resulting from personal sales calls can run into hundreds or even thousands of dollars.

It is this combination of high cost and low rate of response that limits the efficient use of sales forces. However, there are situations where a sales force can prove beneficial and, in some cases, is absolutely necessary. These situations would include but are not limited to marketing high ticket items involving a number of purchase decision makers, products and/or services that are complex and might require demonstration, and companies marketing adopted or "bid-list" materials.

The goal of every good sales staff is to operate as efficiently as possible. That means personal sales calls should be limited to qualified leads or those prospects whose potential for a sale is high. The trick is employing techniques that will effectively qualify sales leads. Depending on the particular circumstances, qualifying leads can range from a simple procedure to a rather complex series of events.

Generating Leads

The challenge in formulating a good lead-generating campaign is to find a balance between the number of leads and the quality of the leads. One can design campaigns to generate high volumes of leads, but often the leads are of very low quality. Naturally, the converse of this premise is also true. Usually the lower the volume of leads generated, the higher their quality or the more likely it is that they will be converted to sales.

The greater the perceived value connected with the least obligation generates the greatest response. Response is reduced as the perceived value drops and as the obligation rises. For example, free promotion literature about a new textbook series is not as attractive as a free copy of the textbook that will sell for $14. The free copy may perform better than free information by perhaps six to one. At the same time, the leads from the free copy offer may convert at one-tenth the rate of those generated from the free information offer.

How does one find the balance between volume and quality? The answer for a $100 product differs from the answer for a $1,000 product, but the principles are the same.

Basically, the more steps in a lead-qualifying program, the better qualified the lead. In addition, the degree of difficulty associated with response is directly related to the seriousness of the responder. In other words, the more difficult it is to respond, the more serious the prospect is in terms of taking action.

There are response techniques that can be employed that will increase the difficulty to respond and serve to help qualify leads. These would include requiring prospects to fill in their name and address on a response device rather than providing this information on a label. Requiring a stamp or envelope be provided for the reply device also adds to the level of difficulty. Eliminating a response device altogether or providing non toll free telephone numbers for response also serves to qualify the leads for a sales staff.

Using The Telephone

Calling leads prior to a sales call is often an efficient method of qualifying the lead. However, keep in mind that in the school market, there are two types of individuals — those relatively easy to reach by phone and those relatively difficult to reach by phone. Principals, secretaries, librarians, and certain district level administrators are relatively easy to reach by phone. Classroom teachers, department heads, and teaching specialists are relatively difficult to reach by phone.

Those leads that fall into the category of relatively accessible by phone should be called. Not by a valuable salesperson, but by a specialist who has good telephone skills. An individual who calls on behalf of a specific sales representative and uses the name of that rep is preferred.

This telephone specialist should open the call with the purpose of making sure that the lead received the information requested. A specialist might also inquire if there's any additional assistance that he or she can offer to the lead.

After seeing that the lead's request has been serviced, the specialist should then attempt to qualify the lead through a series of questions aimed at determining the motivation behind the request for information. Was it a casual attempt to stay up-to-date on new product, or is there a specific purchase being planned? Is it a building level purchase or a district level purchase? Has the funding already been approved or is the program a candidate for the next budget? Is it funded by federal, state, or local monies? How many individuals will participate in the decision? Do these individuals need to receive information?

Through pursuit of answers to questions about the purpose of the inquiry combined with the use of good telephone skills, a specialist can do a great deal to help a salesperson determine on whom to call and when to call in order to optimize selling time. But what about those individuals who are not accessible by phone?

The One - Two Punch: Mail And Inbound 800 Numbers

For those individuals who are not accessible by phone, there are only two alternatives. Either they must be motivated to initiate a call for information or a personal visit must be arranged. Since the goal is to avoid visiting prospects whose buying intentions are not serious, the focus should be on encouraging hard-to-reach individuals to call for information.

An inbound 800 number is usually vital to the success of eliminating poor leads. Asking leads to call collect simply doesn't work. The American public has been raised to believe that one doesn't call strangers collect, particularly strangers trying to sell something.

Secondly, leads see themselves as potential spenders, and the act of calling collect can appear demeaning to them.

In addition, a form letter requesting leads to call a general 800 number will probably not succeed. Remember, the purpose is to become familiar enough with the lead so access is gained to "inside" information that will help to identify a propensity to purchase. This requires a more personal approach.

The best opportunity for success is the use of a personal letter sent to the lead from a sales representative. The letter can be sent to explain that the rep would like to provide additional information such as pricing details, success stories in other areas, or plans on the part of the company to develop supportive products. To increase believability, the letter could explain that attempts to reach the lead by phone have failed.

Those calls that are received for the representative must go through the telephone specialist. And, the specialist must have the means to identify this type of call such as including extension numbers in the outgoing letter. Once a call comes in, the routine is the same as with outgoing calls. Begin by making sure the leads have all the information they need, provide some additional information, and proceed to ask the lead-qualifying questions.

The Best Approach

While space advertising may be one of the easiest ways to generate leads, it poses problems because seldom does a magazine's subscriber base include only the qualified readership that is sought. It is lack of qualification of readership that causes one to limit the response in order to cull out the most qualified respondents.

Direct mail, on the other hand, often allows more control over list selection. If sales people develop and maintain a list of individuals who sit on textbook adoption committees, it might be advisable to mail an offer of a free sample book to that list. It even provides the opportunity to introduce the actual salesperson who will call.

When the readership (or list) is qualified as eligible buyers, the need to hold down the front-end is greatly reduced. More enticing offers with more powerful free gifts can be presented with less likelihood of seeing no return sales.

Consider These Examples

Here is one example of a relatively simple lead generating campaign. Let's assume a company markets hundreds of items and recently mailed its bi-annual, 500-page catalog. A lead-qualifying program may consist of telephoning customers whose sales over the past 6 months exceeded a certain dollar amount. The purpose of this call would be to maintain customer contact by inquiring as to any needs the customer may have and, if one is necessary, schedule a personal appointment. In many cases, an order might be taken over the phone eliminating the need for any sales call.

Perhaps the situation requires a more complex approach. For example, consider a series of high ticket software programs and compatible hardware. A lead-qualifying program might begin with an informational mailing to customers and/or prospects. This mailing might include the entire line, a new product being launched, or a special offer on existing product. Anyone interested in additional, more specific information would be asked to respond via a business reply card.

A second mailing would be sent to all responders. The second mailing would consist of more specific information such as pricing and, possibly, a demonstration disk containing samples from one or all of the software programs. Those responding to this second mailing would request a telephone call by a sales person. The phone call would help to further qualify the sales lead and possibly result in a personal sales call.

Timing

The best policy to adopt regarding response time to inquiries is one of immediate response. This is because respondents have incredibly short memories. Bingo card respondents, in particular, may circle so many information request numbers that they do not have a clear understanding of from whom or why they are receiving promotion literature.

The quality of leads diminishes with time. If the objective is to establish contact to determine whether to send a salesperson, the contact should be as soon as possible after the request for information. After all, at least one and possibly two additional exchanges may take place with an inquiry before a sales call is made. The sooner the response goes out, the sooner the additional contacts can be attempted.

One final point about timing. Response to a new inquiry is an intro-duction to a potentially new customer. Taking a first order from an individual who is annoyed at a lack of responsiveness is not likely to happen.

Stay Focused

Over the years, when discussing creative projects with clients, the request has often been made to produce promotion material that can be used as both a handout by the sales staff as well as a direct mail pro-motion. This approach requiring one promotion piece to accomplish two very different goals is not recommended.

The sales handout should act as a supplement to a personal sales call, summarizing the detailed information discussed during the sales per-son's visit. On the other hand, the direct mail insert is a stand alone piece and must tell the whole promotion story, usually in detail. Experience has shown that in trying to kill two birds with one stone, each bird is merely wounded and neither goal of the dual-purpose pro-motion piece is accomplished. It is much more cost effective to create two separate pieces in order to maximize the effectiveness of each.

Arm Your Sales Force

And that leads to the importance of providing appropriate promotion material for the sales staff. Once again, this material should be designed specifically as a sales handout to enhance the sales presenta-tion. The material should summarize all points covered during the sales visit and not contain superfluous information that may serve to confuse the recipient. It should serve to refresh the prospect's memory regarding the information discussed. It should also contain specific information such as pricing, product specifications, and information on who to contact with any questions.

Once a sales call has been made, if the prospect has still not committed to a sale, further follow-up is advisable in order to maximize the effort and expense of the sales visit. A letter confirming important points discussed during the visit should be mailed in a timely fashion. After the prospect has had time to consider the information, a follow-up phone call is recommended in a last attempt to obtain an order.

Of course, not every sales visit will result in an order. But effectively qualifying sales leads is critical to maintaining an efficient and profitable sales force.

CHAPTER 13

SELLING HIGH TICKET ITEMS

HIGH TICKET ITEMS are products or services that sell for $500 or more. They are difficult if not impossible to sell through direct marketing in one effort. A two-step process often is cost justified and results in the most effective cost per order. This is particularly true when a salesperson is required to close the sale. Using mail to identify good prospects for sales people to call on can significantly improve the cost effectiveness of a sales force. (See Chapter 12.)

Two-Step Promotion Approaches

Two-step promotions can take many forms. The criteria of a successful combination is simply what works for a particular program. The most common forms of the two-step approach are shown in Figure 22.

Deciding which form to try depends on a number of factors, the most important of which are price and complexity of the product or service being sold. In general, the lower the price and the easier it is to explain

193

the benefits of the product or service, the more one might expect to succeed with forms A, B, and C. Conversely, the higher the price and the
more difficult it is to explain the benefits of the product or service, the
more one must employ forms D and E to be successful.

Figure 22

Forms of Two-Step Promotions

Form of Two-Step	Step 1 Lead-Getting	Step 2 Conversion Attempt
A	Direct Mail	Direct Mail
B	Direct Mail	Telemarketing
C	Telemarketing	Telemarketing
D	Direct Mail	Sales Call
E	Telemarketing	Sales Call

It should be noted that there can be major differences in success rates
depending upon which form is employed. Unfortunately, most marketers who use two-step programs seem to evolve into them as a matter of expedience rather than design. A better method would be to test
the different forms available under controlled circumstances and identify which is most effective.

Consider this example. Assign costs and response and conversion rates
for a given program to the forms identified in Figure 22, then calculate
the cost per order based on the various forms that are illustrated. Using
judgement and experience, one might begin with the assumptions in
Figure 23.

Figure 23

Cost, Response and Conversion Assumptions

Lead-Getting
    Direct Mail
        Cost Per Thousand $850
        Response Rate   1.5%

    Telemarketing
        Cost Per Hour $50
        Leads Per Hour   2.0

Conversions
    Direct Mail
        Cost Per Thousand $1,000
        Conversion Rate   5%

    Telemarketing
        Cost Per Hour $50
        Contacts Per Hour   5.0
        Conversions Per Hour   .5

    Sales Call
        Cost Per Call $850
        Conversion Per Call   30%

If the assumptions in Figure 23 are used to calculate net cost per order for each form of a two-step promotion, the results shown in Figure 24 are developed.

Figure 24

Hypothetical Cost Per Order

(Using Assumptions In Figure 23)

Form of Two-Step Promotion	Cost Per Lead	Cost Per Conversion	Total Cost Per Order
A. Mail and Mail	$56.67	$ 20	$1,153
B. Mail and Phone	$56.67	100	667
C. Phone and Phone	$25.00	100	350
D. Mail and Sales Call	$56.67	2,833	2,720
E. Phone and Sales Call	$25.00	2,833	2,628

Calculation Of Total Order Cost

Form A: Mail and Mail. Based upon the assumptions in Figure 23, 1,000 lead-getting pieces are mailed at a cost of $850 and result in 15 leads. At a direct mail conversion cost of $1,000/M or $1.00 each, a $15 expense yields .75 in sales (at a 5% conversion rate). Hence, a total expense of $865 yields .75 sales or a total cost per sale (or order) of $1,153.

Form B: Mail and Phone. The mail lead-getting assumptions are unchanged from case A so 15 leads still costs $850. But with phone, the conversion rate is .5 per hour at a cost of $50. At the rate of 5 contacts per hour, it will take 3 hours to reach the 15 leads or $150 in cost to yield 1.5 sales. Therefore, $1,000 is spent to get 1.5 sales at a total cost of $667 per sale.

Form C: Phone and Phone. The phone lead-getting effort yields 2 leads for every $50 invested on the telephone. To generate 10 leads requires an investment of $250. At 5 contacts per hour it will take 2 hours to convert the 10 leads to 1 sale (.5 conversion per hour). Thus, a total of $350 is required to yield one sale.

Form D: Mail and Sales Call. Using the same mail lead-getting as in Form A, $850 is still required to generate 15 leads. However, now an investment of $850 per sales call or a total of $12,750 is necessary to net out 5 sales (30% conversion rate). Hence the total cost per sale is $2,720.

Form E: Phone and Sales Call. Returning to the same lead-getting techniques as Form C, it is necessary to spend $250 to get 10 leads by phone. At $850 per sales call, the total expense to call on all 10 leads is $8,500. At a 30% conversion rate, an average sale of 3.33 yields a total investment of $8,750 or a cost per sale of $2,628 each.

With the same program, varying only the combination of lead-getting and conversion techniques, there is a difference of $2,370 between the lowest and highest total cost per order. If possible, format combinations should be tested until the right mix is achieved. Keep in mind, the program should make sense. For example, some products or programs simply can't be explained adequately by phone. Use judgement to try the approaches that suit themselves to a particular product or service.

Preserving Conversion Rates

Depending on the nature and price of the product or service, one can expect the process of lead-getting and conversion to take anywhere from several weeks to several years and involve anywhere from one or two decision makers to as many as a dozen or more.

Developing leads is seldom a problem. The challenge is always in developing qualified leads and finding the optimal mix between the number of inquiries and the level of conversion that can be expected. Let's look at some of the different techniques used to control this mix.

A Case History

Company XYZ sells an administrative software package for $1,200. The program keeps track of attendance and grades and often requires hardware investments to accommodate the software. Company XYZ makes lead-getting mailings all year by using a number 10 envelope with personalized letter, brochure, and business reply device.

The lead-getting piece is mailed to school principals, district superintendents, and school board presidents. Each list receives a slightly different version of the letter. The mailings are controlled geographically so that a salesperson may effectively follow-up in a region after leads have been developed from the mail.

Most of Company XYZ's sales are made on a building basis although enough sales are made district wide to warrant a marketing effort to them as well. The challenge in selling the systems comes from direct competition and from service bureaus. The sale seldom takes less than a year and often between one and two years. At least two people have to be sold on the purchase: The buyer or funder (principal or district supervisor); and the user (a combination of the school secretary and the building level computer coordinator).

Because of the difficulty of the sale and the relative expense of the sales call, Company XYZ attempts to qualify the seriousness of their leads on the lead-getting response device. Here's how the response card reads:

> ❑ YES. I want to learn how your software program helps me cut administrative costs while I improve our records and enhance student report card turnaround. Have someone contact me with information on how I can purchase your program for my school.
>
> _____
>
> Signature   Title
>
> _____
>
> Area Code Telephone
>
> You can help us to serve you better by completing the following:
>
> 1. Current Administrative Records
>   ❑   With Service Bureau
>   ❑   On Another In-House Software Package
>   ❑   Done Manually

2. Students Enrolled _____

3. Should You Decide To Purchase Will It Be For
    ❑ This Budget Year
    ❑ Next Year

Company XYZ prioritizes the follow-ups depending upon how completely the card is filled out and the answers that have been provided. The salesperson's assistant calls the responses in order of this priority to book appointments until his or her schedule is filled for a given region. Some responses are not called at all because, based on the lack of information returned, they are deemed poor risks. However, all responses receive, at the very least, a letter acknowledging their inquiry and sales literature on the system's capabilities.

The approach used by Company XYZ could be altered to deliver more inquiries by, for example, promising a free book on the subject of administrative software or management. However, given the relatively expensive selling cost associated with the conversion process, more leads are probably less desirable than better leads.

For those marketers already involved in a two-step promotion technique (or that suspect they should be), design a few tests to make sure the process currently being used is best for the particular situation. If the lead-getting piece currently includes substantial qualifying information, lower some of the requirements and see what happens. If it doesn't qualify, try some of the qualifying techniques suggested in this chapter.

Designing Promotions For High Ticket Items

If you were planning to buy an expensive piece of jewelry, chances are the first stop on your shopping list would not be the local discount store. Bargain basements are not where most shoppers would begin their search for that perfect wedding dress. This is because while price is almost always a factor, large, significant purchases carry with them a certain aura of importance. When spending large sums of money, the buyer needs to feel that he or she is receiving a reliable product of high quality. Promotion material should reflect this quality image and avoid a "clearance sale" approach.

In the education market, most decisions regarding purchases of high ticket items involve more than one individual. In many cases, after reviewing information a committee will make a purchase recommendation that then requires approval at the district level or by a board of education. Promotion material must appeal to a variety of individuals each with his or her own set of interests and priorities.

Often, high ticket items such as computer hardware or products related to new technology are complex pieces of equipment. This can make the operation and/or benefits of a product or service difficult to convey. However, the promotion material should be clear, concise, and easy to peruse. Complicated product descriptions and unfamiliar technical terms can be a serious deterrent to generating interest in the promotion message and should be avoided.

As previously discussed, selling high ticket items through a single mailed promotion is not easy and may not be the best approach.

Effectively appealing to a variety of people, explaining complex technology, describing a variety of benefits, and justifying a large expenditure usually proves to be too much for one promotion piece to accomplish. For large ticket items, the recommended approach is a multiple mailing, perhaps coupled with a personal sales call.

The purpose of the first mailing is to generate interest in the product or service. Depending upon the complexity of the information that needs to be conveyed, this promotion could take the form of either a direct mail package or selfmailer. Keep in mind that it is not necessary nor recommended to tell the whole story about the product at this point, but simply generate enough interest for the recipient to request more information.

The first mailing should contain a brief, non-technical description of the product or service. It should also include benefits that will appeal to the variety of individuals that may be involved in the purchase decision. Pricing at this point is usually not included, especially if pricing is complex involving many levels and/or peripheral equipment. And, as previously mentioned, the quality and style of this promotion should be compatible with the product's value.

Consider 4-color processing, heavier paper stocks, and simple, clean typefaces. Avoid dense copy blocks and employ the use of heads and subheads to encourage scanning of the material. Leaving plenty of room or "white space" between elements of a promotion of this type will subliminally serve to make costly items or complex products less threatening.

If it is advantageous to qualify the leads from the initial mailing, consider these techniques. Require prospects to fill in their own name and address on the return request form rather than supplying it for them on a mailing label. Require prospects to provide their own postage. Ask that prospects write or call for more information and do not provide any response device. The more difficult it is for prospects to respond, the more serious their request for information. And the more costly the follow-up techniques (i.e., personal sales call), the more qualified the leads should be. After all, the goal is to limit any visits by the sales staff to serious requests.

It is common for requests for information from an initial mailing to be followed up by a second mailing. Again, depending on the complexity of the information to be conveyed, a direct mail package or self-mailer format could be used. While this mailing should include a more detailed description about the product or service, the design should be compatible with the first mailing and maintain a sense of quality and dependability. It is advisable to indicate on the outside of the piece that it includes information that was requested which can enhance deliverability and readership.

In come cases, a request for an order is included in the second mailing. For products or services that are more complex or costly, telephone follow-up or a personal sales call is usually necessary. Once again, the method by which the prospect requests a sales call will help to qualify the lead.

CHAPTER 14

THE CHALLENGES OF FUND-RAISING

THE ACTIVITY OF fund-raising relates to those products or programs that schools or their organizations promote to raise monies for support of school programs or activities. Promoting fund-raising programs presents unique challenges to education marketers.

Successful Fund-Raising

Suppliers of fund-raising merchandise and services face a competitive battle for success. It is a challenge to establish and maintain unique products and services as numerous companies offer the same or similar fund-raising items. For example, M & M candies and gummy bears are in almost every catalog along with tee shirts and mascot imprinted items. Even donkey-ball suppliers, where service distinctions are difficult to identify, face stiff competition.

To make matters worse, the circumstances surrounding the selection of fund-raising programs often inhibit buyer awareness and customer loyalty. In many cases the final selection is a semi-democratic process often involving a vote by students. A company's reputation for service doesn't carry much weight among this group of trend-oriented consumers.

Finally, most districts and school buildings have adopted a policy of fund-raising program "management." Generally, this translates into a practice of prohibiting two identical programs by competing student groups in the same season. For suppliers of fund-raising programs, this is a difficult policy under which to maximize sales.

In summary, selecting a fund-raiser is a complex decision-making arrangement which includes district and building policy along with limited advisor intervention over student voting. The result is a reduction in a fund-raising company's ability to provide product or service distinctions. Because the number of schools participating in programs can fluctuate from one season to the next, the lead-times and fixed costs associated with setting up manufacturing lines can be prohibitive.

Stand Out In The Crowd

In the face of these conditions, what is a fund-raiser to do? When the product or service is not unique, one must make a sales argument in other major business areas such as customer service, packaging, and promotion. If it is not possible to enjoy the luxury of holding an exclusive on a particular program, then one should be sure that the programs offered are available, timely, and attractive.

Customer service can be a significant way of distinguishing a company from the competition. Guaranteeing fast turnaround time on orders is a distinct benefit - especially to a group of "now"-oriented young people. "All orders shipped within 48 hours or your merchandise is half-price!" is an attractive claim. If operating on a 100% mark-up, the only liability with this type of guarantee is the shipping and promotion cost.

Another attractive claim is to guarantee a cheerful replacement or complete refund if the end user is not satisfied with the merchandise. The incidence of redemptions should be extremely low but the level of confidence created by such a guarantee can be quite high.

Other distinctions can be created through services such as credit terms, inbound 800 ordering lines, WEB sites, service hotlines, and outbound shipping options. Credit terms can be extended based on credit references and authorized signatures in lieu of the time-consuming purchase order. While this adds some logistics and expense on the part of the fund-raising company, it greatly reduces the time barriers for respondents.

While inbound 800 numbers are fairly common these days, service hotlines are not. To a number of school groups the ability to know just where their order is and when it will ship can be quite valuable. Especially if the group is behind schedule or the victims of a prior bad experience. And in the case of seasonal programs such as Christmas and Easter for example, an express shipping option (at an extra charge, of course) may be a factor in deciding which fund-raising company a group selects.

Fund-Raising Offers That Motivate

Packaging is also an unexplored opportunity in school fund-raising programs. In apparel programs, one often sees shirts, shorts, and hats for sale but seldom a set of all three with incentive pricing or a free item tossed in. In the case of candy sales, which are a major source of fund-raising revenues, it would seem that the "happy meal" concept has possibilities. One package of Reese's Pieces, one M & M's, one Gummy Bear combined with a free trinket all for a special price is an example.

Some companies package free freight into their pricing while others charge for freight and add free merchandise based on the volume purchased. However, experience has shown that in most cases, neither free freight nor free merchandise is as motivational as the conversion of their value into discounts.

While much focus has been given to developing attractive graphics for fund-raising programs, relatively little has been given to exploiting promotion concepts. No doubt, the complex decision-making process, seasonality, and constant change in popular items makes testing difficult. But, it's not impossible.

A number of companies have enjoyed success with premium programs. It raises the question of the possible success of bonus point programs or longer term premium programs that benefit the school or district similar to the old Green Stamps or current Campbell soup type programs. Bonus point programs offer some hope of conquering customer loyalty problems.

Build A Database

Mailing lists represent yet another promotion challenge (and opportunity) for fund-raising companies. Most companies maintain a jumbled in-house file of customers and inquiries, but few really have an understanding of just who the individual is on the file. Unlike many other education lists, the major database compilers do not maintain most class and student group advisors by name.

This puts most companies in a position of mailing their customer file by name and, in many cases, again by title if they are using a compiled list of titles. This strategy does not serve to enhance customer relations. However, the dilemma is correctable with some planning, forethought, and patience.

First, establish a database that is building oriented. Second, obtain the advisory position that is held by the name on the customer file. With these two pieces of information it is possible to control who is being mailed by name or title.

To accomplish these goals, add name-gathering techniques to a fund-raising promotion. For example, supply a list of titles and ask the respondee to fill in the names of the school advisor positions listed. Reward them with free merchandise if they complete the information. Eliminating duplicate promotions to individuals and mailing prospects by name should improve the impact of fund-raising mailings.

A further step would be to incorporate a numbering system into the customer database that would allow the elimination of duplicate school buildings with one of the major list compilers. This capability could virtually eliminate duplication between customer file and prospect mailings and perfectly generate one promotion piece for those advisors known by name and another by title for those whose names are not available.

Fund-raising is by no means an easy business in which to succeed. The fundamental job of selecting, stocking, and managing product, even though the same or similar products are offered by competitors, is still a challenging art. But to rely on product alone in a highly competitive environment invites the opposition to gain an advantage through customer service, packaging, and promotion techniques. The hard fact of fund-raising is that one must stay in the forefront, not just to succeed, but to survive.

Magazine Sale Survey Results

When carefully conducted, surveys can often provide information that can aid in targeting a market and motivating a response. A recent survey regarding magazine fund-raising sales was sent to approximately 9,000 schools, 1,400 of whom responded. Highlights of the survey results include the following:

• About half of all magazine sales were school-wide while the other half were conducted by groups within the school. However, of those group sales, 90% were conducted grade-level wide.

• Eighty-four percent of all magazine sales were conducted between late summer and fall.

- Almost three-quarters of all sales run for two weeks or less.

- Sixty-one percent of all sales grossed under $11,000.

- Eighty-four percent of all sales earned profits of between 31% and 40%.

- Less than 12% of all sales earned profits greater than 40%.

Several of the questions asked in the fund-raising survey reveal attitudes and habits that are useful to all fund-raising marketers. Figures 25 through 29 illustrate the results of these questions.

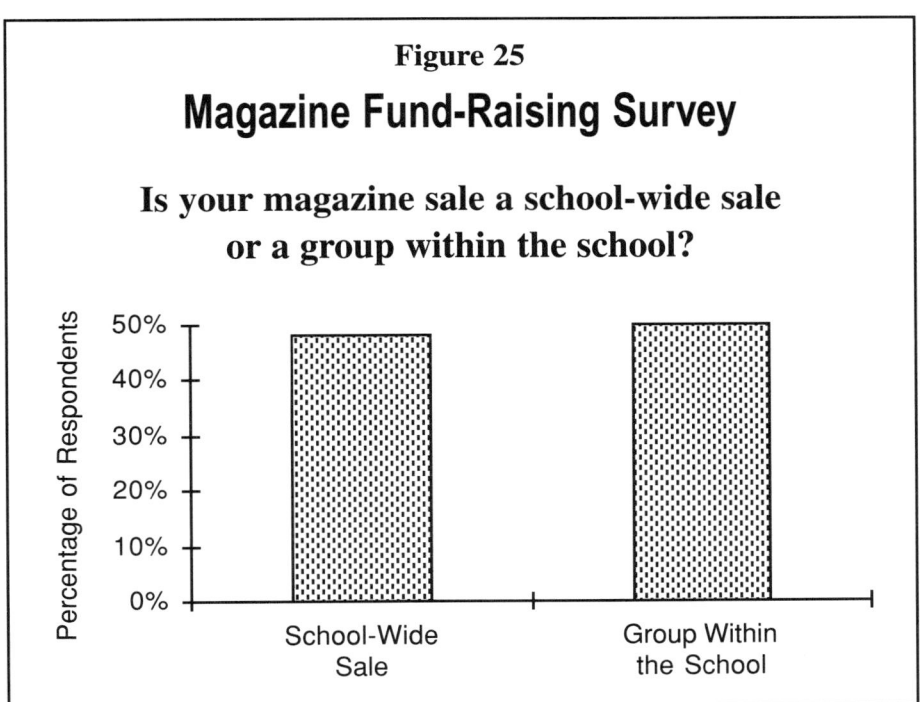

Figure 25

Magazine Fund-Raising Survey

Is your magazine sale a school-wide sale or a group within the school?

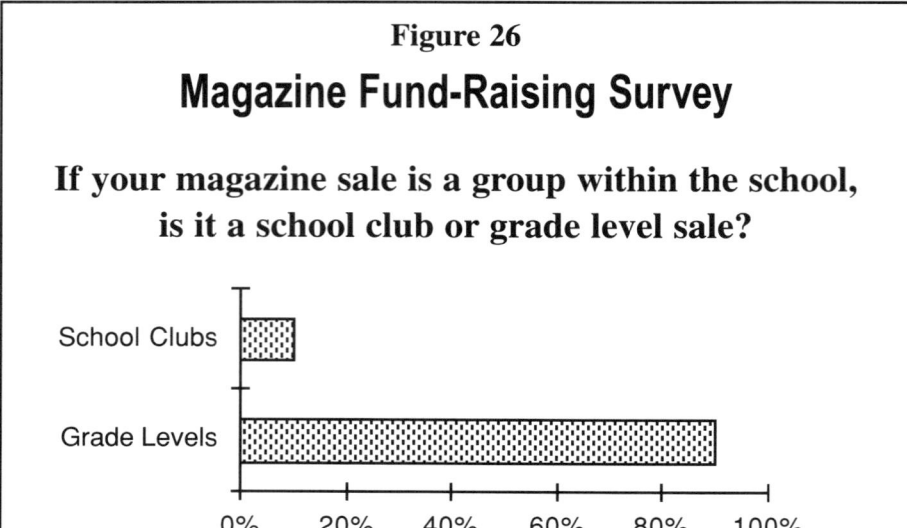

Figure 26

Magazine Fund-Raising Survey

If your magazine sale is a group within the school, is it a school club or grade level sale?

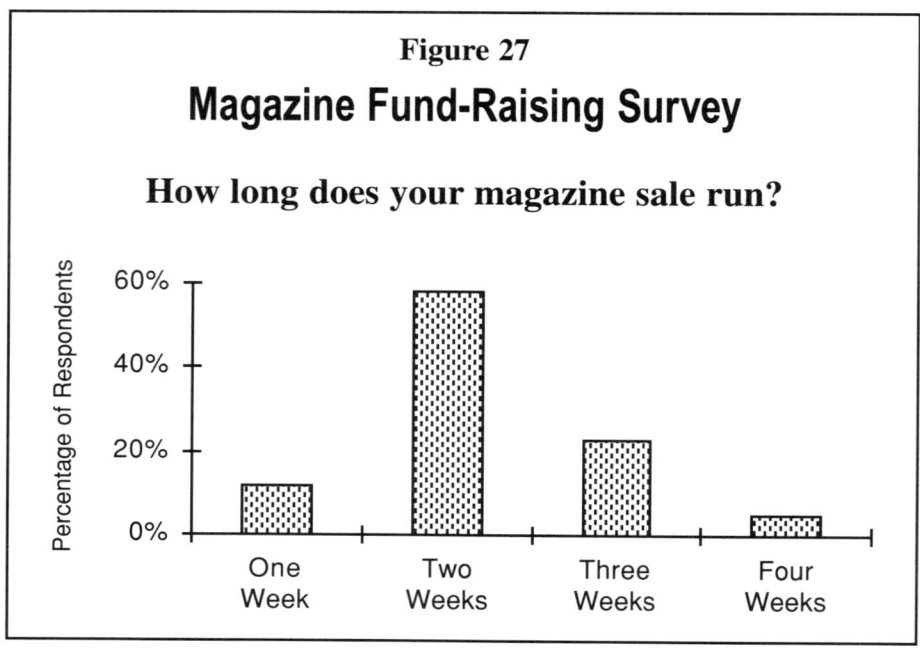

Figure 27

Magazine Fund-Raising Survey

How long does your magazine sale run?

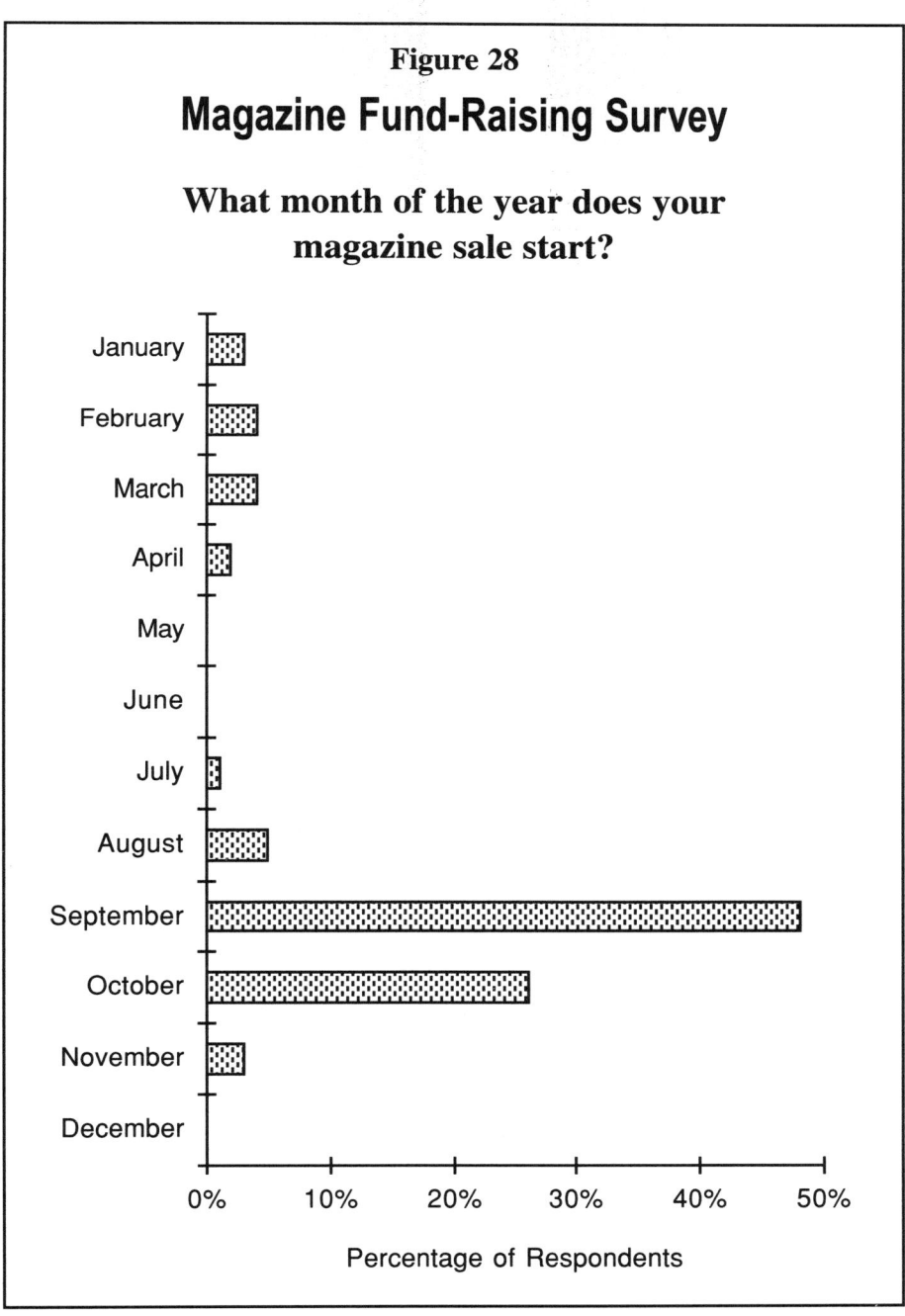

Figure 28

Magazine Fund-Raising Survey

What month of the year does your magazine sale start?

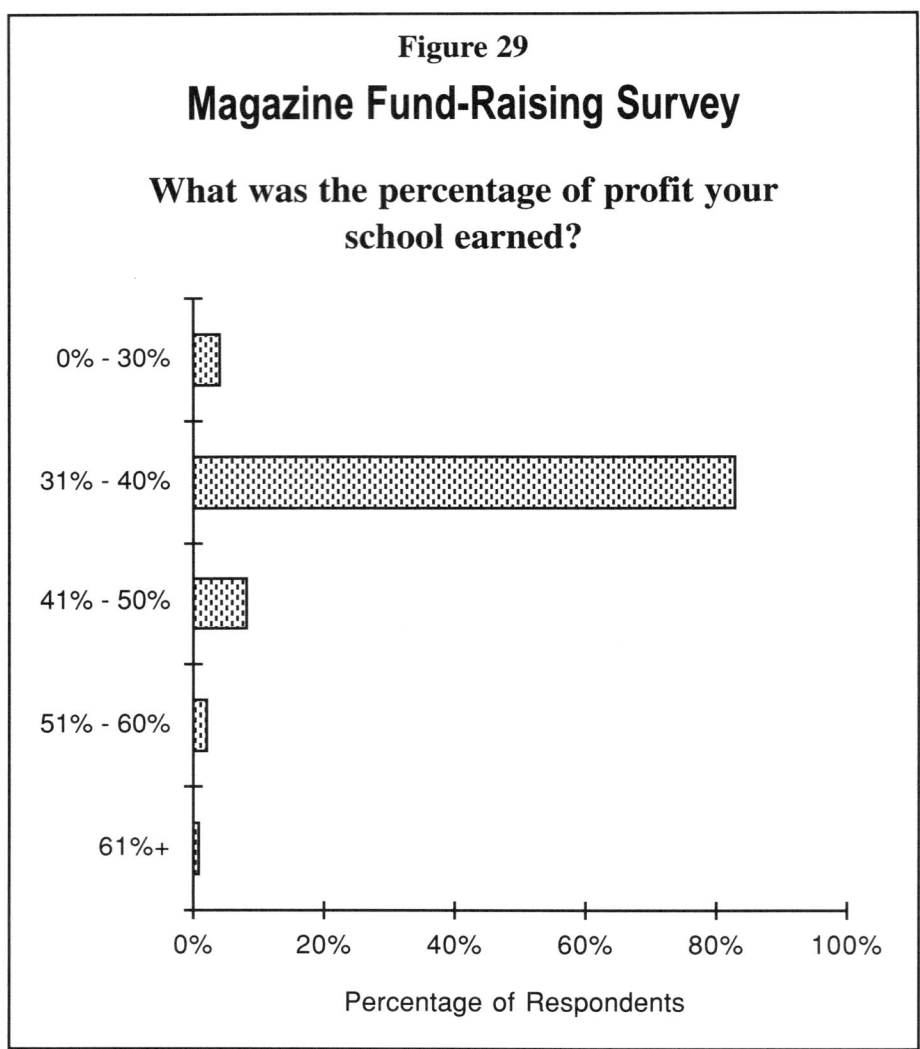

Figure 29

Magazine Fund-Raising Survey

What was the percentage of profit your school earned?

CHAPTER 15

PROS AND CONS OF USING DISTRIBUTORS

MANY EDUCATIONAL MARKETERS supplement their direct sales through distributors. For some educational marketers, sales through distributors can be 50% of total revenue or more. To determine if using distributors is a viable option, consider the pros and cons.

The Case For Using Distributors

There are a number of benefits to using distributors. For example:

1. Distributors tend to sell to a certain type of buyer, one that is not likely to be captured with a direct selling effort.

While this opinion is based upon experience with numerous companies that use distributors, it may not be as obvious to marketers who have no experience with them. Logic suggests that if there is one vendor for a given product and one outlet from which it is purchased, the addition of distribution or other outlets must infringe on sales that would otherwise be direct.

However, experience shows that while this is a logical notion, it is not representative of what actually happens in the marketplace. The reality is that even though a specific product may not be available elsewhere, some reasonable substitute for that product is often available. So even if Joe's Math Workbook is not available through a distributor, they do carry Jane's Math Workbook.

For most products, buyers prefer to purchase through the outlet with which they are most comfortable; and, in many cases, are willing to make reasonable product substitutions. It is easier for buyers to substitute products than it is to change buying habits. They would rather continue buying through a retailer or distributor with whom they have established a relationship than buy direct from a company with whom they've never done business.

The exception exists when the product is not easily substituted, although very few products fall into this category. However, even when the product does not have a reasonable substitute, it will take considerable time and investment to convert retail and distributor buyers to direct buyers.

Why should this be so? Consider the nature of the buyer. The customers of distributors may have one of several characteristics that make them difficult to convert to direct sales. The retail buyer (teacher store customer), may be an individual who prefers the hands on, immediate delivery aspects of retail purchasing. This type of individual is not a particularly good prospect for mail order sales.

Some buyers like the one-stop shopping convenience that large distributors afford them. Others view the products listed in a large distribution catalog as being somewhat endorsed by the company. Their rationale is that if the product wasn't any good, it wouldn't be in their catalog.

Still others buy from distributors because the distributor has won the school or district bid. In fact, they are captive buyers who couldn't buy direct with school funds even if they preferred that method.

Research into buying habits among classroom teachers revealed an interesting set of statistics. When asked whether they bought at teacher stores or through mail order catalogs, one third of the teachers responded that they bought through catalog only; one third said teacher store only; and one third said they bought through both channels equally. Since many distributors publish and mail catalogs as well as maintain teacher stores, the incremental market share that can be available from distributors could be from one-third to one-half of the market.

2. Distributors can significantly increase the production runs for products. These production efficiencies can positively effect the cost of product for direct sales as well.

Most products cost less to produce as the volume increases. Doubling sales through distributors can have a significant impact on product costs. These cost deductions apply not only to distribution sales, but to direct sales as well. In fact, some manufacturers and publishers use distributors for this reason alone.

Depending upon the product, a single distributor can have a major impact on a business. A large school supply company or a retail chain can move tens of thousands of units of some products with little more than a listing in their catalog or placement on their shelves. To sell the same volume through direct sales could require a substantial promotion investment.

3. Distributors bear the majority of their own cost of sales, making sales through distributors relatively cost free.

For most companies, the largest cost in distribution sales is in the initial acquisition of the distributor. But once a distributor account has been acquired, cost of sales drops dramatically and the cost to service the account is what remains.

Most distributors expect good service from the manufacturer/publisher. This would include availability of inventory, reasonable payment terms (at least net 30 days), and that the manufacturer/publisher stand behind its products by replacing goods returned due to defects in manufacture.

Catalog distributors also expect some graphic arts support for catalog pages whether it be film, camera-ready art, or a fiscal allowance for same. Depending upon the nature of the product line and the availability of promotion materials, some distributors expect a supply of the manufacturer/distributor's own catalog minus the address so the distributor can imprint their own address. They also expect the manufacturer/publisher to make these catalogs available at cost or, in some cases, below cost.

Many manufacturer/distributors already have these materials available to support their direct business. Often distributors make a commitment to bear the distribution cost of the materials they are given. Consequently, the selling costs through a distributor are relatively low compared to those incurred in direct selling efforts.

The Case Against Distributors

The case against using distributors is more an examination of the complexities of working with distributors than it is an argument against using them entirely. The major challenge is in the area of marketing strategies. Distributors do not appreciate special offers, such as discounts or premiums, that are made directly to customers through mail order efforts in which the distributor is not allowed to participate.

In fact, unless the product is a strong seller, some distributors will refuse to do business if the manufacturer/publisher pursues separate, direct marketing strategies. It's my opinion that, in most cases, distributors actually benefit from these programs. However, experience shows that most distributors do not share this view.

On the other hand, manufacturers who decide to only develop marketing programs in which the distributor can participate, may find themselves frustrated and limited. The frustration stems from the fact that dealers often cannot share in the cost of discounts or premium programs. The distributor is hampered by the 50% cost of goods which limits promotion investment. This same 50% discount from the suggested retail price hampers the manufacturer/publisher as well. There just isn't a lot of money left for promotion efforts.

There are few marketing programs that can work for both the manufacturer and distributor. One program that offers a chance for success is a rebate offer.

Launching A Rebate Program

USA Today has reported that close to 80 billion dollars worth of rebate coupons were distributed by American industry over the course of a year. Less than 3% of that amount was redeemed. That means that American business enjoyed $80 billion in promotion play at a cost of $2.4 billion or 3¢ on the dollar. That's a good promotion investment by any measure.

How much of that was distributed by school marketers? Hardly any at all. Why not? Because the school market is a marketplace of followers. The overriding opinion seems to be that if the competition doesn't do it, it must not need to be done. These circumstances make for a unique opportunity in the school market. And as is usually the case, the first companies to take advantage of these circumstances will enjoy the greatest rewards.

Marketing through education distribution channels - whether through retailers or catalog dealers - is uniquely complicated. The first major challenge arises when goods are offered to distributors at approximately 50% off the selling price. This alone imposes severe restrictions on a producer's ability to provide *profitable* and *effective* marketing incentives. On the other hand, this 50% cost of goods imposes equal restrictions on a distributor's ability to provide these same incentives to educators.

The result is a world devoid of significant marketing incentives. So much so that some marketers draw the conclusion that incentives don't exist because they aren't needed. Nothing could be more wrong. And the development of good marketing incentives was never so critical to education marketing as it is today.

Unique Advantages Of Rebates

Rebates provide a high impact, low cost solution to the dilemma of marketing through distributors. They allow manufacturer/publishers to provide affordable incentives to dealers. And they can be reasonably controlled and managed by the manufacturer/publisher.

A rebate is a specific dollar amount promised to the end-buyer by the manufacturer/publisher. The buyer must furnish proof of purchase and a rebate coupon in accordance with the manufacturer/publisher's published policies. In between the promotion message announcing the rebate and the actual rebate itself is a significant percentage of procrastination on the part of the buyer that results in no rebate being issued. The degree of this lack of redemption varies based upon the level of difficulty required to redeem and the amount of the rebate.

Keep in mind that as one limits the amount of the rebate and makes it more difficult to redeem, one also reduces the attractiveness of the offer and its ability to enhance sales. Personal procrastination and the difficulty of getting rebate coupons through the educational bureaucracy go a long way toward controlling rebate expense.

Step 1: Choose A Popular Product

No amount of good marketing will make a bad product succeed in the long run. The opportunity for success is greater if incentives are targeted at more popular products.

All products do not need to be included. The ideal circumstance is when a product line experiences an average order of several units. By attaching a rebate to one unit, one may anticipate several other units to be bought at full price.

Here are several types of rebate offers:

1. $X off on purchase of a specific product.
2. $X off on any title or item among a specific family of products.
3. $X off on a set of (2 or 3 or whatever makes sense) products.
4. Whatever has a potential for success!

Step 2: Keep It Simple

Keep the promotion simple for both the end buyer and the distributor. Develop promotion materials that incorporate the rebate program and offer them to dealers in a manner consistent with regular promotion materials. For example, a stuffer or promotion flyer and/or a catalog insert could be created. Produce only a rebate version or consider producing two versions — one with a rebate and one without. If it makes sense, build the coupon into the promotion page. In other cases, it may be better to provide the coupon separately.

The important thing to remember is to keep the policy with regard to promotion allowances to dealers consistent with any regular policies. This will cause the least confusion and provide the best chance for participation.

Step 3: Make It Easy To Order

The most successful programs are often also the easiest in which to participate. Require proof of purchase, use an expiration date, and provide instructions on how to redeem the coupon. Use easy to understand language and make the redemption process easy. There's plenty of opportunity for procrastination on the part of the buyer if they are simply required to show proof of purchase and return the coupon. Those requirements should be sufficient.

Step 4: Promote The Program

The whole idea of a rebate program is to draw attention to products through rebates so it is important to fully promote the program. If a space advertising budget exists, advertise the program. Promote it at dealer trade shows and through a sales force. One of the major opportunities a rebate program affords is promotion play so it pays to advertise it heavily.

If the first program doesn't succeed as anticipated, don't give up. Rebate programs require a certain expertise. A first attempt with no prior experience can have disappointing results. But don't declare rebates a failure. The product, the rebate dollar amount, and/or poor execution of the program could contribute to poor results. Conduct a post-mortem and try to establish a likely cause for any disappointment. Then correct it and try again. Persistence will greatly enhance the chances for success.

CHAPTER 16

MAINTAINING A CUSTOMER FILE

CUSTOMERS CAN BE one of the best sources of revenue for almost any company. Unfortunately, many school marketers do not maintain sufficient records of their customers. Some feel it's a waste of time, others believe it's not worth the expense, while still others continually relegate this project to the "back burner." This chapter offers a few suggestions to ensure that the maximum benefits are being obtained from a customer file.

What Good Is A Customer Name?

Most marketers do a thorough job of prospecting, making sure that seasonal promotions mail on a regular basis. But it is surprising how few do a thorough job of mailing special promotions to existing customers. It is incredibly important that customers be promoted on a regular basis, because those promotions usually result in high rates of return.

Marketers who are proficient at tracking their results have known for years that customers order in magnitudes five times or greater than do prospects. Often mailings that are a failure or only marginally successful when mailed to the universe can be profitable when mailed to customers.

If a company maintains a good relationship with its customers and offers appealing items at attractive prices, it ought to be able to succeed with several promotion attempts to those customers over the course of a year. It's not likely that the same mailings made to prospect lists will succeed as often.

When strategically planning school market promotions, a popular goal is to attempt a break-even approach when prospecting to build the largest customer base from which to develop profits. While many school marketers execute prospecting strategies competently, they often miss the mark on customer strategies.

Often this marketing faux pas is excused based on the rationale that since customers cannot be deduplicated from prospects, why bother making a separate mailing? The fact is that the customer mailing should be special and unique to customers only and mailed in addition to prospecting efforts.

Why It Should Work

Customer mailings are profitable because of a number of factors. First and foremost is the fact that the mailing goes to the best possible list a marketer could select -- active buyers.

Second, customers recognize the names of the companies from which they buy and usually receive their promotions with enthusiasm. Consequently, because the mailing goes to active buyers, the promotion format does not have to be terribly elaborate for it to receive attention. This can result in lower promotion costs.

Thirdly, experience shows that customers will act at response rates significantly higher than prospects. However, and this is critical, customers should be given a reason to act now, as opposed to whenever they'd like. In addition, prior experience should show that the products or services customers are offered are in demand.

The concept of a customer promotion may be likened to a renewal rate for subscription products. Circulation managers realize that unless they can pull a fifty percent renewal rate or better, they probably don't have much of a subscription product. This is not to suggest that a customer mailing will pull fifty percent. But the response rate of a customer mailing that is several times the response of a prospect mailing is normal. When a correctly conceived and executed customer promotion does not pull three to five times better than a prospect promotion, it's a clear signal that there may be problems with the product offering.

How Much Is A Customer Worth?

Different approaches have been developed over the years to place a value on a new customer. Outlined here is a very simple method that can be embellished to fit a particular business situation.

The following information should be readily obtained from a customer file.

> Average order size.
> Number of customers who repeat in year 2.

Assume an average order size of $300.00 and that 70% of the customers repeat from one year to the next. Each of these customers are worth, in gross revenue, the following amount:

Year 1	$300.00
Year 2	$210.00
Year 3	$147.00
Year 4	$102.90
Year 5	$72.03
Year 6	$50.42
Year 7	$35.29
Total	$917.64

If the cost of goods is 50%, then the average customer is contributing half the gross revenue or $458.82 toward promotion expense, overhead, and profit over his or her lifetime.

The major expense over the life of this customer is the initial acquisition cost in year 1. This amount is something that can be calculated as well by taking the promotion expense and dividing it between customers and prospects.

For example, a $5 catalog is mailed to 60,000 customers annually, while a mini-catalog is mailed to 100,000 prospects each year. If 70% of the customers repeat, the acquisition cost for them is the total promotion cost of $300,000 divided by the number of repeat customers of 42,000 or $7.14 each. The prospects cost $100,000 to mail and, if the prospect mailings pull a 2% response, yield 2,000 orders. Consequently, the acquisition cost of prospects is $50.00 each.

Roll these numbers out over the life of the average customer and the scenario in Figure 30 will result:

Figure 30

Customer's Value Over Time

Year	Order Acquisition Cost	Average Gross Revenue	Average* New Revenue	Contribution** to Overhead and Profit
1	$50.00	$300.00	$150.00	$100.00
2	7.14	210.00	105.00	97.86
3	7.14	147.00	73.50	66.36
4	7.14	102.90	51.45	44.31
5	7.14	72.03	36.02	28.88
6	7.14	50.42	25.21	18.07
7	7.14	35.29	17.65	10.51
Total	$92.84	$917.64	$458.83	$365.99

* After 50% cost of goods.
** Average net revenue less order acquisition cost.

Given that each customer order costs $7.14, spending $50 to convert a prospect to a new customer yields $365.99 over the life of that customer toward overhead and pretax profits. If the overhead runs 20% of revenue and the customer file is 60,000, that generates a little over $1.5 million per year in pretax profits. The following figures summarize this example:

Lifetime Contribution to OH and profit per customer	$365.99
Lifetime Overhead	$183.53
Lifetime Pretax Profit	$182.46
Average Pretax Per Year	$26.07
Total Based on 60,000 Customers	$1,563,943.80

How much is a particular customer worth? That depends upon a number of factors. Following the model that is outlined in this chapter will provide a good starting point from which to determine the value of a customer. And this exercise can also help to add more confidence when making day-to-day promotion strategy decisions.

Start With The Vital Statistics

Once the decision has been made to maintain a customer file, it is necessary to determine what information will be included. It's fairly obvious that a customer file should contain an address. What may not be so obvious is that the file should also contain the name (and the title or grade level if possible) of the purchaser in addition to the name of the institution.

Who Is The Customer?

The purchaser or customer is defined as the individual to whose attention the product is shipped, not the individual who receives the bill. In most cases, the "ship to" person is the decision maker, while the "bill to" person is simply a paperwork processor. However, there are exceptions to this rule.

Many school supply companies receive purchase orders which contain several names. This information usually contains one "bill to" name and address and anywhere from one to a dozen "ship to" names and addresses. The customer is the individual who initiates the order.

If the supplies involved are paper clips, paper, staples, pencils, and other supply-type items, the customer is most likely the "bill to" name and address. If the order is for teaching materials, learning games, workbooks, software, video, film, or filmstrips, the customer is most likely to be the "ship to" name and address.

Most institutional orders have only one address, where the "bill to" and the "ship to" individual is the same. But a significant number of school orders have two different addresses. Due to constraints in the computer systems used to maintain customer files, some companies must choose between maintaining the "ship to" names or the "bill to" names on purchase orders. Forced to choose between one or the other, it is recommended that the "ship to" names rather than the "bill to" names be maintained on the customer promotion file.

The logic for this decision is as follows: If forced to make the choice, it's easier to find alternative mailing strategies to reach "bill to" names than it is to reach "ship to" names. For example, if a marketer rents names from a list house that are not maintained on the marketer's file, it's much easier to rent the universe of district level business agents and purchasing managers. This file is only 16,000 names and is likely to encompass many of the names that would be included in the "bill to" file. To try to rent names equivalent to a "ship to" file might include the entire universe of teachers which could exceed a million names.

In many marketing situations, response can be improved by mailing to a name rather than a title or institution. When designing order forms, make sure the order information includes a line for the name of the individual making the purchase along with his or her job function followed by a line for that person's school or institution. When orders are placed via inbound telephone, train operators to ask for this information.

It is also recommended that a phone number be included in a customer's record whether or not telemarketing is part of the promotion strategy. First of all, it doesn't take much to add a line requesting a phone number on an order card nor is it a lengthy bit of information to add to each record. And, if a decision is made to call customers for whatever reason, it can save significant expense in telephone number look-up charges.

Profile Customers

After the vital name, address, and phone number statistics have been gathered, add some information with which to profile the buyer. For example, include what has been purchased. If only a few products are marketed, this could include the actual product. If a variety of products are offered, perhaps the information would be limited to the product group or division from which the purchase has been made. Keep in mind that the more specific information, the better the customer profile. This purchase information will make it possible to send specific types of promotion materials to specific types of buyers.

Maintaining the actual amount of the purchase in the customer file is also recommended. This includes dollars and may also include quantity if applicable. For example, quantity purchased could be helpful when promoting an ancillary product that would only be appropriate for those customers who have purchased a particular quantity in the past.

Perhaps one of the most important pieces of information to maintain is when the purchase took place. It is not necessary to maintain a customer on file indefinitely. Basically, a customer's potential for future purchases decreases in proportion to the length of time from last purchase. In other words, if a customer hasn't made a purchase after a certain length of time, prospects for future purchases from this individual are dim.

A rule of thumb is that any customer who has not purchased anything for a period of three years should be considered an "inactive" customer and classified as such. Not only will this procedure ensure that a streamlined and efficient customer file is maintained, it will also eliminate the expense of mailing to "dead wood" during any promotion efforts.

For some product lines, a three year cut-off date is not appropriate. A particular situation may require that a customer be maintained for a longer or shorter period of time and that's perfectly acceptable. However, there comes a point in time in almost every business when a customer is no longer profitable to maintain on an active customer file. At this point it should be transferred to an expire file or a file of ex-customers. This file should be maintained by the date of the last order that was placed (i.e., one-year expires, two-year expires, three-year expires, etc.).

Customer Files Help To Analyze Business

In addition to keeping the information for promotion purposes, there is another useful aspect of a customer file. That is the ability to gather information pertinent to one's business. It is possible to draw from the information maintained on a customer file to generate reports that can help analyze many different aspects of a business. This information can be very helpful when making future decisions.

The reports that can be created are really limited only to one's imagination and budget. Here are some suggestions for the kinds of information that may be helpful:

Average order size, either in terms of quantity, dollars, or both, can be helpful in determining what direction to take to increase average order size or when developing pricing for product.

Maintaining the most frequent order amount in quantity and/or dollars is also recommended. For example, do the majority of orders fall in the $5 to $10 or $25 to $30 range? Do customers purchase 1 to 5 sets or 50 to 100? This type of information can be used when planning future marketing strategies, pricing, and product configuration.

A report that indicates sales by product and/or product line or group can be critical. While sales may have increased by 200% over last year, this report can indicate which product(s) contributed the greatest percentage of increase and which may be candidates for elimination in the next promotion cycle.

Customer service questions can be addressed through information found in a customer file. For example, is the average shipping turnaround time reasonable or is there room for improvement? The percentage of returns as well as what is being returned and why can be determined. A customer file can be a wealth of marketing knowledge as well as opportunity.

A Customer File Can Be A Source Of Additional Revenue

Another aspect of the customer file is the ability to generate revenue by renting the names of one's customers to other marketers. In fact, some companies actually break-even or lose money on their promotion efforts simply to gather customer names because leasing these names is so lucrative.

Of course, renting one's customer names to direct competitors is not recommended. Ask to see a sample of the promotion piece that will be mailed to the customer file. If the piece is promoting math workbooks and your company markets playground equipment, there is minimal risk in renting the names.

There are those who argue that renting customer names results in their customers becoming deluged with promotion materials which spoils them as good buyers. But there is another school of thought that says the more direct mail sent to direct mail buyers, the more practiced they become at purchasing through this medium.

Including selection options in a customer file usually makes the list more attractive and can generate additional revenue. For example, dollar amount of purchase, number of times purchased, secondary vs elementary level, name vs title, and geography are selections that are desirable and for which charges can be added over and above the base price to rent the file.

There's More Than One Way To Maintain A Customer File

When implementing a customer file, there are several options from which to choose. However, before considering the options, it is a good idea to begin by listing any specific requirements.

Items to consider are the number of records that will be maintained and the length of each record. Determine the number of reports that will be generated, the contents of each report, the information that will be used to create each report, and the frequency with which each report will be generated. None of these items has to be cast in stone, but by initially determining this information, it will aid in determining the best method of maintaining a customer file for a particular situation.

First, there are several database management packages currently available, many of which can be used on IBM PC compatible equipment. For a relatively low cost, the hardware and software necessary to maintain a customer file and generate reports can be purchased. Keep in mind that these systems usually have their limitations regarding the number of records that can be maintained and the speed with which they process information.

There are also database management companies that will maintain a customer file and generate reports for a fee. If considering this option, inquire about any minimum billing requirements. These companies will also, in some cases, perform only the data entry function. Then a tape or disk of the information is sent to the marketer from which to generate reports, labels, or invoices.

Creating Customer Promotions

When creating customer promotions, there are some characteristics that are unique to this type of mailing and should be considered.

A popular format for customer promotions is the four-page, 11" x 17" sheet folding to 8 1/2" x 11". It is relatively inexpensive to produce, can be mailed without an envelope, and still leaves plenty of room in which to sell. However, there are other formats that can also work well.

The correct amount of product per promotion is very much a function of the nature of the product. For example, a four-page flier is not required to sell pencils. Everyone knows what pencils are and, if they are attractively priced, a smaller format should be successful. Software, on the other hand, might easily require a four-page flier to describe its features in an easy-to-understand manner.

As a general rule, the more commonly understood the item, the less selling space can be allocated without detracting from response. On the other hand, the more complicated or new in concept a product is, the more selling space may be required. The main point to keep in mind is that a customer promotion should do significantly better than a prospect promotion. Therefore, a less expensive format should generate an acceptable response at a much lower promotion cost.

Selecting Product

There are two types of product offerings which have proven most successful for customer promotions. One is high volume, popular product, particularly if it is consumable material. The other is either absolutely new product or new versions and follow-ups to popular existing product.

Many marketers would prefer to attempt to sell slow moving items or even non-moving items, but these tend to result in a poor customer promotion or one which yields little or no profit. Products that are not easily sold through normal marketing channels will probably not move well among customers. The possible exception is if they are offered at an extreme price cut as in a clearance sale.

The Offer Is Always Critical To Success

A customer offer should provide motivation to act now. This is why an offer is most effective when positioned as a special that will not be available forever. When creating customer promotions, one can gear the offer to customers only and lend credence to the "special" aspects of the offer.

Most school marketers that mail regular customer promotions report success through price discounts. An assortment of discounted items is presented with large discounts on some items and small discounts on others. Some items are at full or close to full price to allow a decent overall margin in the product mix.

Creating The Customer Promotion Theme

It's a nice touch to create a theme for a customer sale because it gives the recipient a context in which to accept the sale and lends the whole promotion credibility. Suggestions include a "back-to-school" sale, a "warehouse clearance" sale, a "Christmas" sale, a "holiday" sale, an annual "customers are terrific" sale, or just about anything that comes to mind.

Sales with product themes are also a possibility. For example, a "teacher's aids" sale, a "duplicating master" sale, an "office supply" sale, and so forth. And, of course, both concepts can be combined as in "teacher's aids warehouse clearance" sale or "duplicating masters holiday" sale.

Opening Salvos

Customer promotions need not dawdle in getting to the point of the promotion. Rather than open with pretty covers or high impact graphics as a prospect promotion might, get right to the selling in a sale promotion, or right to the critical benefits in a new product promotion.

It's important that customers find it easy to order. Here are some basic terms and conditions that will help a customer promotion succeed:

Payment: Extend credit terms. Remember, these are customers and they have qualified themselves as good credit risks. Many school marketers think they are extending credit by asking for a school purchase order number. Technically speaking, they are. But a purchase order number cannot be assigned impulsively and impulse is a big part of direct response. A "bill me" option allows the customer to order now and do the paperwork later.

Guarantees: Always guarantee any product completely. Even if individuals have purchased from a particular company in the past, they need to know they have recourse in the event there is a problem with a product or the new product that is offered is not what a customer envisioned from the promotion. Lifetime guarantees are recommended or, at the very least, a thirty-day guarantee.

Minimum Orders: If absolutely necessary, add a handling charge for small orders. But never refuse to do business with a customer just because their order isn't large enough.

Returns: Avoid threatening copy that requires approval for returns.

Instead, invite returns as part of the guarantee and simply tell the customer to call for prompt return instructions.

Telephone Orders: Encourage them. If concerned about the validity of the order, call the school back under the guise of checking the address and inquire as part of the check whether the ordering individual is employed there.

Prices: Use an expiration date for the sale and guarantee the prices to that date. "Prices subject to change without notice" negates the effect of the sale.

Timing

Customer mailings can follow regular mailings (made to both prospects and customers). They are additional opportunities and can be dropped in the mail anywhere from 2 weeks to up to 2 months after a major mailing. Figure 31 illustrates mailing window opportunities associated with customer mailings.

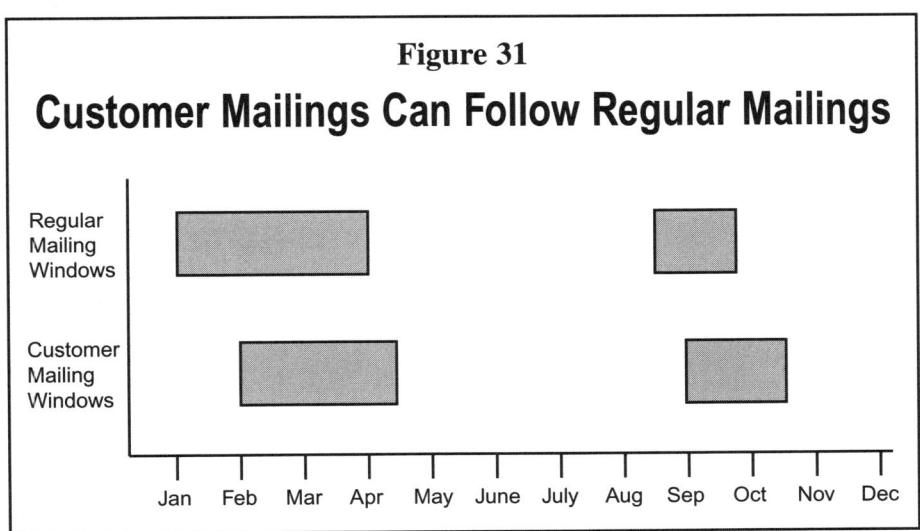

Figure 31

Customer Mailings Can Follow Regular Mailings

Regular Mailing Windows

Customer Mailing Windows

Jan   Feb   Mar   Apr   May   June   July   Aug   Sep   Oct   Nov   Dec

CHAPTER 17

TESTING AND TRACKING

SO MANY IMPORTANT things to learn—so much expense and effort to learn them. Should a discount be used? Do premiums work? Is a free trial offer better than a preview offer? What's the best price? Which list works best? Testing, including the ability to read the results of tests, is one of the most challenging aspects of school marketing. This phenomenon is one of the characteristics that sets the school market apart from other forms of direct marketing.

Envy the marketer who works with teachers directly and receives the original response device rather than a purchase order over 80% of the time. That person can answer a variety of marketing questions in a single mailing because of the ability to track results. But the institutional market offers a unique challenge in that it's not unusual to receive only 10% of original order devices or less. While techniques have been developed to help reduce the problem of tracking results, perfect solutions can be expensive, often involving redesign and replacement of one's entire fulfillment system.

Management By Opinion

Unfortunately, without testing there is never any progress. Marketing decisions are based on opinions. This method of decision-making usually leads to the same result: The person with the largest salary or holding the majority of the stock often has the most compelling opinion regarding the direction of future marketing efforts.

To progress and fine tune future marketing efforts, the results of past efforts must be reviewed. Analyzing the data from past promotions is the only method by which qualified marketing decisions capable of improving results can be made. In addition, the data must be dependable. No opinion can overcome reliable data regardless of salary levels or number of shares held.

There are a few simple approaches that have served school marketers well for years. While short of perfect, when applied with discipline, patience, and perseverance, these approaches can help to gather a significant amount of marketing information without incurring unreasonable costs.

Creating A Test

There are five major components of response that hold opportunity for improved results. They are list selection, offer composition, timing, format selection, and copy and design presentation.

List selection can have the greatest impact on response and is one of the easier tests to administer. The most successful technique is to add a department code into the return address. Using an inkjet address process, a unique department code can be assigned and printed in the return address for each list. The school business office includes the department code when addressing their purchase order and the data is captured when the order is entered. Most school marketers report tracking 30% - 60% of their response using this technique.

Offer tests are more difficult to administer. Each school building has its own demographics that influence its propensity and ability to buy. Few school marketers have been successful in selecting control and test panels that are comprised of schools with equal demographics.

The most effective technique to accomplish demographic equality is by dividing the marketplace of schools and districts in half, separating the odd from the even zip codes. This will also yield approximately equal numbers of schools and teachers.

One of the more reliable techniques is to use item codes unique to each test panel. In order to avoid havoc with computer and inventory systems, most companies choose to develop prefix or suffix codes that are only visible in their sales reports. Thus item 101 becomes 101A in the test, 101B in the control panel and 101C in the balance or bulk portion of the mailing. The drawback to this technique is that it adds considerable expense to create test panels using this method. Also, the most effective use of unique item codes is limited to catalog mailings.

Discount pricing, use of premiums, or rebate programs are concepts that can also be tested. Others might include free trial offers, money-back guarantees, and the extension of billing privileges to institutions.

Two Methods Of Tracking

Assume a premium structure is being tested to determine its effect on sales. The test will be conducted only in the New England area. Mailing lists are ordered in the following three lots:

Lot 1: The Premium Version - includes all the even zip codes in New England.

Lot 2: The Control Version - consists of all the odd zip codes in New England.

Lot 3: The Bulk Version - consists of the balance of the mailing to the rest of the nation.

The promotion package for Lot 1 (the test group) carries a suffix to all item codes of A, Lot 2 (the control group) carries a suffix to all item codes of B, and Lot 3 (the bulk) carries a suffix to all item codes of C. When the orders come in, sales are tallied by the item code suffixes and results are calculated.

This example actually contains two methods of testing: 1) assigning unique item codes and 2) segmenting by sectional center. While the alternative method of odd vs even sectional centers does a good job of isolating sales by geography, it is less desirable due to the fact that sales cannot be separated from prior promotions. This is especially true of catalog promotions which can generate long term carry-over sales. Therefore, test results could be skewed by orders received from other promotions.

These two methods of testing (prefixing and suffixing item codes and splitting out odd and even sectional centers of a like geographic area to form control vs test and test panels) deliver the highest rates of trackable business. Keying order forms, using unique post office boxes or department numbers, including pressure sensitive labels the respondent is asked to affix to the order form, and inkjet addressing directly to the order form are alternative methods of tracking tests, but are not nearly as accurate.

Evaluating The Results

The first step when evaluating test results is to tabulate key data. For each control and test group it is important to know total promotion expense, total sales dollars, and total cost of goods. The most commonly collected data is listed in Figure 32 . This data is used to create calculations that help to evaluate performance as listed in Figure 33.

The best way to evaluate results is to do a contribution analysis. A contribution analysis begins with total sales less cost of goods. The result is called contribution to promotion, overhead, and profit. From this, promotion cost is subtracted and the result is called contribution to overhead and profit. Finally, overhead is removed and the result is profit. Figure 34 illustrates a contribution analysis calculation.

The advantage of the analysis in Figure 34 is that it allows promotions to be considered with respect to their total net effect on business as well as incrementally to the base business.

Figure 32

Tracking: Data Collected

Promotion Volume: How much was mailed?

Promotion Expense: How much did it cost?

Number of Orders: How many responses?

Dollar Value of Orders: What are they worth?

Source of Order: What promotion generated the order?

Figure 33

Tracking: Data Calculated

% Response = Number of Orders ÷ Promotion Volume

Promotion Cost Per Thousand (CPM) =
    Promotion Expense ÷ No. of Thousand Pieces Mailed

Promotion Cost per Exposure (CPE) =
    Promotion Expense ÷ Total Readership

Cost Per Order = Promotion Expense ÷ No. of Orders

Average Order Size = Dollar Value of Orders ÷ No. of
    Orders

Figure 34

Contribution Analysis

Gross Sales $

- Cost of Goods

_____

= Contribution to Promotion,
  Overhead, and Profit

- Promotion Cost

_____

= Contribution to Overhead and Profit

- Overhead

_____

= Profit

Evaluating Media: An Example

In order to evaluate a test, consider the data listed and defined in Figure 32. This data enables the calculations listed and defined in Figure 33 to be made. Among these calculations is the "bottom line" or determining factor in test evaluation which is cost per order. Some mailings cost more than others. Some deliver more orders than others. The common ground evaluation is cost per order. Consider this example:

A marketing manager promotes a new program through two different mailings. One is a direct mail package consisting of an outer envelope, brochure, letter, order form, business reply envelope, and a publisher's note. It cost $750 per thousand to mail and generates a 3% response.

The other effort is a selfmailer. It costs $300 per thousand to mail but generates only a .5% response. Which promotion is more cost effective?

Solution To Example

Here is the mathematical solution to the example:

Direct Mail Package

Cost/Thousand = $750
% Response = 3.0% or .03
Orders/Thousand = 30
Cost/Order   = Cost/Thousand ÷ Orders/Thousand
            = $25/Order

SelfMailer

Cost/Thousand = $300
% Response = .5% or .005
Orders/Thousand = 5
Cost/Order   = Cost/Thousand ÷ Orders/Thousand
            = $60/Order

The direct mail promotion is the winner. Even though it cost more to produce and mail, its increased response yielded a per order cost that was almost 60% lower than the selfmailer.

Patience And Perseverance

Testing and tracking are not easy in the school market and require great planning and patience. The difficulties associated with testing often cause business to be conducted as usual -- never really challenging the many issues faced by school marketers. But by using some of the techniques mentioned in this chapter, some important questions can be answered and, over time, marketing efforts can change for the better.

CHAPTER 18

DATABASES AND MAILING LISTS

BY FAR, LISTS exert the most influence on response rates over the other components associated with a promotion. Figure 35 illustrates just how influential lists can be when compared to the other components.

Figure 35

Influence Of Various Components On Response Rates

Component	Influence On Response Up To
List	1000%
Offer	500%
Package Format	100%
Timing	50%
Copy and Art	30%

School and educator mailing lists represent a unique resource in school marketing. In an industry that generally lags behind in marketing techniques, school marketers are fortunate to have available for use the most advanced databases that have ever been created. These powerful resources have been developed over time through the efforts of many individuals in an attempt to improve their ability to reach the marketplace.

A Brief History

Not too long ago, major educational mailers maintained their own lists. Most were compiled from state directories published by state departments of education. That's how Dr. Forrest Long, founder of Roxbury Press and a Professor of Education at New York University compiled his lists. The year was 1928, prior to the invention of the computer, so Dr. Long maintained his lists on addressograph plates.

As other school marketers learned of these lists, Long began renting them as a favor. Over time, as his list business grew, he added a lettershop and service bureau. Eventually he began to compile lists related to the education market including health care and churches. Today, Dr. Long's company is known as Mailings Clearing House located in Sweet Springs, Missouri, and is still owned and operated by the Long family.

In 1968, about 40 years after the founding of Roxbury Press, Herb Lobsenz founded Market Data Retrieval (MDR). Lobsenz had been employed by Xerox Education Publications and had conducted research that involved the collection of school expenditure data. This project led him into the business of renting school data.

In 1982, MDR implemented an agreement with what is now the Weekly Reader Corporation to take over the compilation of their teacher names. MDR made these teacher names available on the list rental market and, for the first time in history, school marketers could rent from a comprehensive list of classroom teachers.

Prior to the agreement with Weekly Reader to make teacher names available, MDR purchased a company called Curriculum Information Center (CIC) that compiled the names of district level administrators. The person who was responsible for the CIC database was Jeanne Hayes. Hayes left CIC and MDR in 1980 and, with some help from National Business Lists, founded Quality Education Data (QED) in Denver, Colorado. QED marketed a database of schools to compete with MDR but with a twist. They were the first to offer in-depth technology selections.

Shortly after Hayes left MDR, John Hood was hired from Baker and Taylor to replace her where he rose through the ranks to become second in command at MDR. In 1990 Hood left MDR and joined CMG Information Services (CMG). Although CMG had been primarily a college list compiler, Hood developed a K-12 database to compete with MDR which included teacher names.

In 1992 Hood added what he called the District Demographic Index (DDI) at CMG which was the first "off-the-shelf" regression model in the school market. In 1993 CMG introduced their "Teachers Who Respond" file which was the first shared response database in the school market.

When QED offered a teacher by name file in 1997, the school market had three sources of lists of teachers by name and four sources of lists of schools and key administrators. 70 years after Dr. Forrest Long started maintaining his addressograph plates, some of the most accurate databases exist for school marketers.

Compilers, Brokers, Managers

Compilers are companies that research school directories, then mail and telephone school districts and buildings in order to create a file of schools, school demographics, administrators, and teachers by name. Compilers know their files and products better than anyone else.

In the school market, the compiled files that are available are the most sophisticated in existence. Schools and teachers can be selected by over 60 different selection criteria – an overwhelming choice of options.

Compiled files offer the advantage of understanding the nature of the schools which they contain. This information includes the size, grades taught, public or private status, size of budget, and much more. The disadvantage to using compiled files is the inability to determine whether or not they contain direct mail responders.

List brokers are professionals whose job it is to know all the list sources available in a given market. Based upon the broker's years of experience and relationships with clients, they should be able to recommend multiple list sources that have some track record in the marketplace. A list brokerage typically uses compiled files and response files in any given mailing. This gives their clients the advantage of combining important information about school demographics with responsive direct mail users lists.

List managers are professionals who help rent a company's list to other mailers. Typically, the list manager markets the list and manages the production and billing. The list owner approves all rentals and reviews all promotion samples to eliminate competitors. In addition to providing extra revenue, many companies who rent their lists find this to be a source of information about what products and offers succeed with their lists.

Building Penetration Strategy

A compiled file offers a number of selections that enable the mailer to implement a ***building penetration strategy***. This means that promotion investment can be controlled by district or school based upon school demographics, the demographics of the community in which the district or school is located, or a combination of numerous district and school characteristics collected by the compiler.

District and school demographics are often defined by census data overlays onto district and school files. These may include combinations of data (i.e., median household income, single head of households, college graduates, etc.), or they may be derived from Federal funding programs (i.e., percent of students qualifying for free lunch program). Most compilers offer several choices and these selections are given names (i.e., neighborhood lifestyle selector, student need indicator, etc.).

In addition to demographic data, there are many district and school characteristics that may be selected. These include school type (public or private), grade span (K-3, 4-6, K-6, K-8, K-12, 6-8, 7-9, 9-12), school enrollment, expenditure per pupil, presence of certain programs (special education, title programs, magnet programs), presence of certain technologies (computer types, VCR's, cable TV, networks, telecommunications), and much, much more. One of the challenges in working with compiled files is understanding which criteria to employ when developing building penetration strategies because there are so many from which to choose.

A simple example of a building penetration strategy is to invest more promotion in schools that are larger or that spend more money. One might choose to mail 100% of the appropriate personnel in large or high spending schools, 50% in medium size or medium spending schools, and one piece per school in small or low spending schools.

Actual sales experience can be used to help develop a building penetration strategy. A customer file can be matched to a compiled file in order to penetrate the buying districts and schools deeper than the prospects.

Personnel Selection Strategy

In addition to a building penetration strategy, a personnel selection strategy can also be productive. First identify which buildings to mail. Then determine the amount of promotion investment. Finally select the individuals to receive the mail.

When selecting personnel, there are two levels of decisions to make. First, choose the appropriate job function. This could be a district level or building level administrator (i.e., curriculum coordinator or school principal); or it could be a classroom teacher by grade level or a teaching specialist (reading teacher, special ed teacher).

After the appropriate job function has been defined, consider the list type. First, there is the house file (customers and inquiries), as well as the most recently updated names to the compiled files (new names). In addition there are direct mail buyers that match the compiled files, the balance of names from the compiled files, and outside lists (or the customer lists of other school marketers).

A Unique Approach To List Selection

One of the most responsive segments of compiled files is a list selection entitled "new teachers." The term "new" means any teacher whose record has been altered on the file. A new teacher could be new to the profession, new to the school, or new to the grade. A new teacher could be one re-entering the profession or recently married with a name change.

But new names represent only about 15% to 20% of the universe. So after using new names, SMRI's strategy was to distinguish between those schools on the client's customer file and those that were prospects. More promotion was then sent to teachers in the customer schools than in the prospect schools.

This strategy worked well enough for a number of years, but it used MDR files almost exclusively. Although other compilers had match programs that made it possible to distinguish customer schools from prospect schools, MDR had the only name file as well as the only new name file.

When CMG introduced their own "Teachers Who Respond" file in 1993, it was the first shared response database. Tests showed that these files represented an additional mailing opportunity. This discovery led SMRI to test specific outside lists on the rental market such as Education Center Buyers, Delta Education Buyers, Bureau of Education Research Buyers, and so forth. These outside lists made up yet another additional source of potentially productive names.

As a result of this extensive list testing, SMRI developed a new list selection strategy. It used MDR as the base compiled file, selecting all new names. Then CMG direct mail buyers were added. The next step was to split the MDR database into customer and prospect schools with customer schools selected more heavily than prospects. Finally, appropriate outside lists were added to the mix. Figure 36 illustrates SMRI's experience of which lists are most responsive.

Figure 36

Which Lists Are Most Responsive?

This list reflects our general experience in order of most responsive to least.

1. Current Customers
   Most recent buyers in a house file.

2. Previous Customers
   All older buyers in a house file.

3. Recent Inquiries
   Inquiries over the last year.

4. New Names
   Teachers new to the profession, new to the school, or new to the job.

5. Direct Mail Buyers
   Other companies' customers, including response databases and outside lists.

6. Other Teachers in Buying Institutions
   The remaining teachers after customers, inquiries, new names, and direct mail buyers in schools with whom business is conducted.

7. Other Teachers in Non-Buying Institutions
   The remaining teachers after inquiries, new names, and direct mail buyers in schools with whom business is not conducted.

When CMG developed its teacher by name files, SMRI began experimenting with CMG's new teachers. There was little duplication between the CMG and MDR new names resulting in another addition to the number of productive lists.

The Duplication Factor

Any database or, in fact, any list of educators by name is a picture of the market place over time and up to the moment that the last record was updated. It is physically impossible to update every teacher in every school at the same moment in time. Consequently, no list is "real time." The only portion of a list or database that is closest to being "real time" is that which was most recently updated. But since lists are not updated in any universal or common sequence, the portion of each list that is closest to being "real time" differs.

Therefore, when the new names or most recently updated records are selected from different sources (MDR vs CMG), the duplication of names between the two files is very low, usually under 15%. The same is true when direct mail buyers are added, whether from shared response databases or outside lists. Most of these are active files and represent the most recent portion of the total house file of the contributor or renter.

Name vs Title

The debate over mailing to a specific name vs a title constantly rages in the education market. SMRI has found that, when the balance of a file is selected and the new names and direct mail buyers have been selected, it is often preferable to mail the remainder of the file by title rather than name. However, the name is rented so that the correct number of titles to generate can be determined.

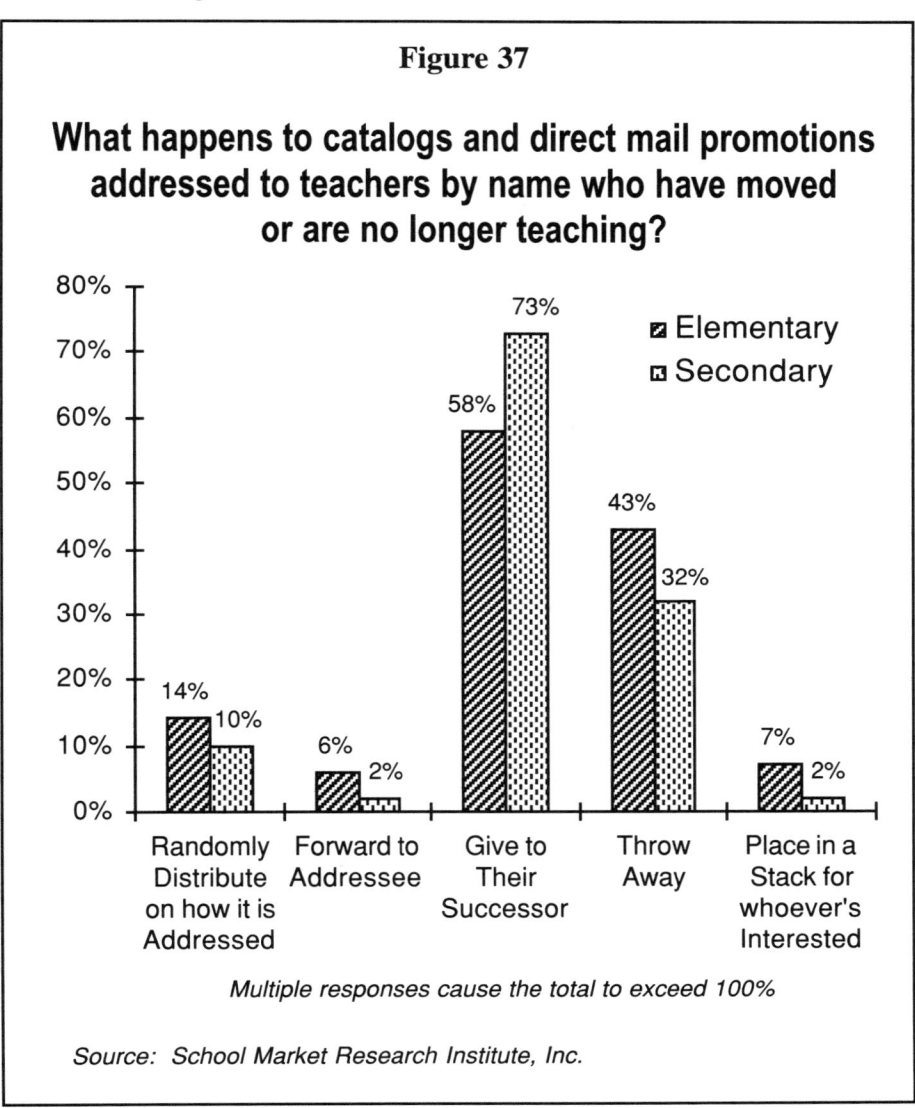

Figure 37

What happens to catalogs and direct mail promotions addressed to teachers by name who have moved or are no longer teaching?

Multiple responses cause the total to exceed 100%

Source: School Market Research Institute, Inc.

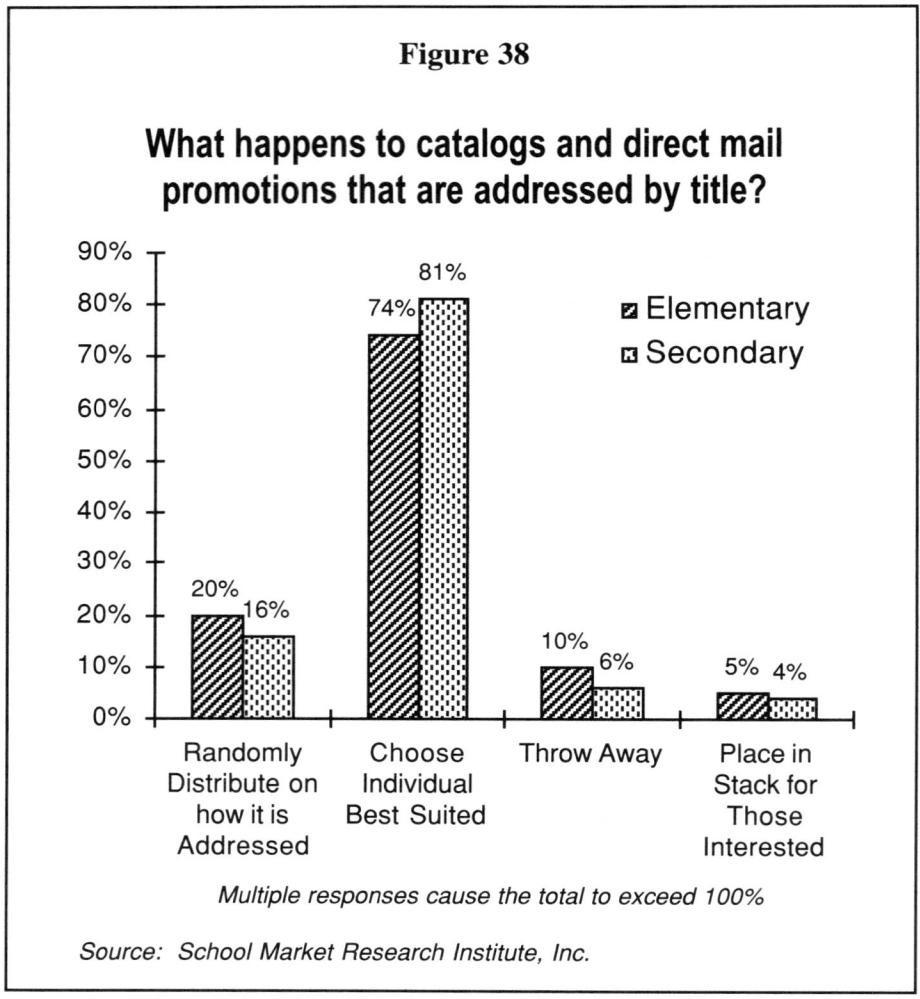

Figure 38

What happens to catalogs and direct mail promotions that are addressed by title?

Multiple responses cause the total to exceed 100%

Source: School Market Research Institute, Inc.

The logistics of mailing to a title rather than a specific name may not be immediately apparent and deserves an explanation. SMRI has conducted surveys of school secretaries. The results of these surveys indicate that when secretaries receive mail addressed to a name, they faithfully deliver it to the name. But when they receive mail that is title-addressed, they "choose the individual they think is best suited to receive it." In other words, they find the buyer. Figures 37 and 38 illustrate the way school secretaries deliver mail when addressed by name or title only.

Consequently, SMRI's strategy is to first mail the most responsive names (the house file, new names, and direct mail buyers) by name in order to put the promotion material in their hands. Then the name is suppressed and the balance of classroom teachers are mailed by title so that the school secretary will find the person most likely to respond.

Explore The Possibilities

Today's successful school marketers do not limit themselves to one list source as this would eliminate too many additional opportunities. Multiple sources are used in order to maximize productive mail volumes. In addition, rather than mailing once each year, promotions are mailed as often as they prove productive. A direct marketing rule of thumb states that if a given mailing delivers a certain rate of response, the same mailing to the same list mailed four weeks later will generate about half the rate of response of the first mailing.

Assume a required response rate is 1% but the list selected delivers 2%. Mailing the same list a second time four weeks later should deliver half its original response rate or the required rate of 1%. Keep in mind that in any mailing, some lists are very productive, some are marginal, and some are not productive at all. Identifying the most productive and remailing them is a way to expand a mailing's universe.

There are several approaches that may be used to call the more productive segments of a list. One technique is called regression model-ing. You can create an evaluation of districts, zip codes, or school buildings using census track data, sales history, or both. You assign weight to each element in your model and then array your lists from best to worst. Depending upon the performance of a list from the first drop, you would decide where to establish a cut-off, mailing only that portion of the list that was ranked high enough to perform satisfactori-ly in a remail. Simpler techniques can be used as well. Certainly cus-tomers can be mailed more frequently than prospects to deliver an acceptable return on promotion. By the same token more recent cus-tomers perform better than older ones. Figure 39 lists several criteria commonly used to identify more responsive list segments. Figure 40 shows a typical remail pattern.

Figure 39
Criteria For Identifying More Responsive Segments Of Lists

- Regression Model (Zip Code)

- Customer vs Prospect

- Recency
    As a Customer
    As a Teacher

- Known Direct Mail Buyer

- List Source

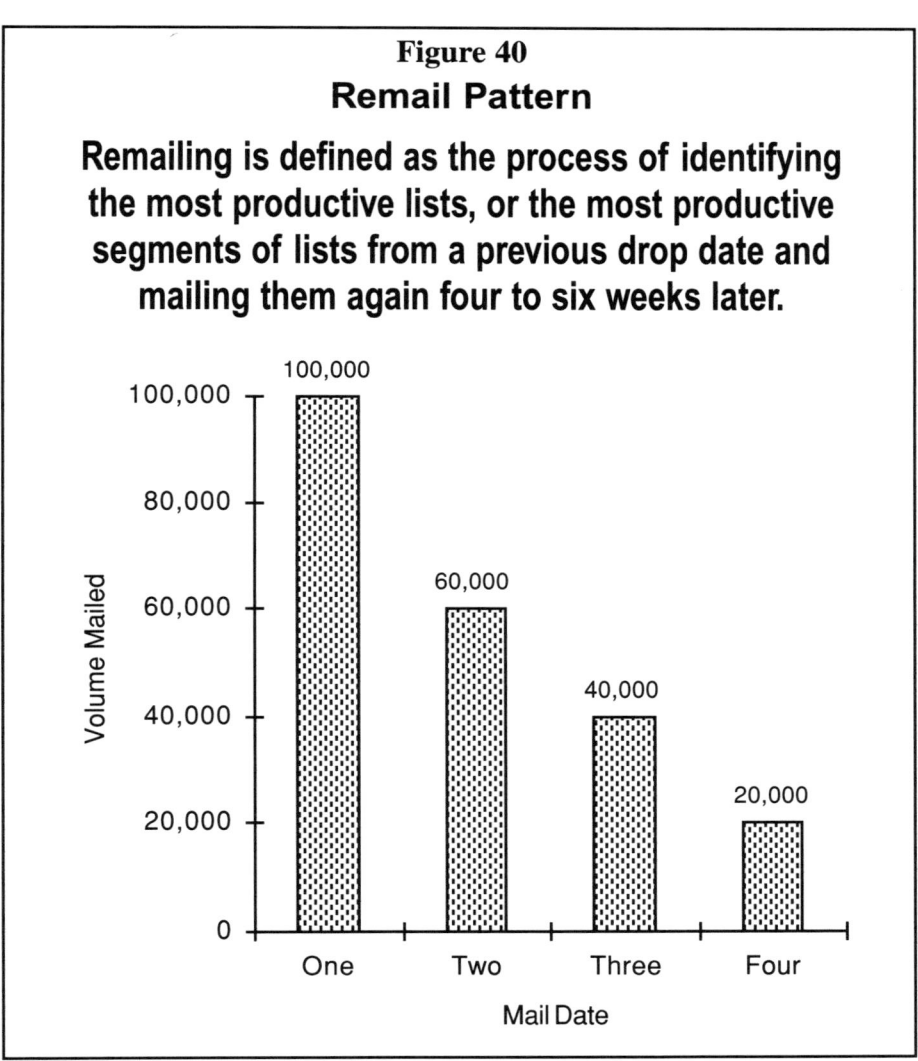

Figure 40
Remail Pattern

Remailing is defined as the process of identifying the most productive lists, or the most productive segments of lists from a previous drop date and mailing them again four to six weeks later.

Educational mailing lists and an understanding of how to maximize their contribution continue to evolve. Improvements in list tracking are accelerating this knowledge. The major compilers continue to develop new products for experimentation. List selection is an area with great potential to contribute to a mailing's success and deserves careful attention.

GLOSSARY

Affixed postage: Postage that is physically applied to a mailing piece such as a postage stamp or meter receipt.

Average order size: The total number of dollars in sales from a given promotion divided by the total number of orders collected. A mailing that generates $10,000 in sales from 100 orders is said to have yielded an average order size of $100 per order.

Back-end response: The total net paid response or number of paid orders from a mailing.

Bad debt: Revenues accrued and lost as a result of lack of payment by customers.

Bingo card: A postage-paid response device included in magazines allowing readers to request further information about material advertised in the publication. Also known as a reader service card. It often contains a large array of numbers, each representing a specific advertiser. The reader circles the number representing the advertiser(s) from whom additional information is desired.

Body copy: The detail copy in promotion literature.

Break-even point: The point at which revenues less cost of goods equals all other expenses for a given program or product line.

Building level purchase: A purchase where the decision to buy was made within a school building without input from the school district.

Bulk: The largest mailed portion of a promotion campaign, separate from test and control vs test panels.

Cash offer: The requirement of payment with an order whether by cash, check or credit card.

Catalog: A multi-page, multi-product offering of sufficient heft (paper thickness) or thickness (number of pages) to be categorized by the recipient as a catalog. A catalog begins at a thickness of somewhere between 16 and 28 pages and continues up into several hundred pages. As the number of pages approaches 200, catalogs tend to become less mail order/direct response vehicles and more like reference books.

Classroom level purchase: A purchase where the decision to buy is made within a classroom (usually by a single teacher) without input from a building-level or district-level administrator.

Control vs test panel: The portion of a mailing equal in volume to the test panels that represents the last previous control or most successful promotion effort. This portion is isolated to provide a standard against which to compare the test panels.

Cost of goods: The cost associated with producing and stocking product. It often includes manufacturing, bulk shipping, and inventory carrying costs. It often excludes developmental costs and the cost of shipping product to customers.

Credit offer: The extension of billing privileges to a school or individual usually allowing 30 days to pay.

Database lists: A comprehensive collection of related data, usually computerized and organized for convenient access. In the marketing field, this term most commonly refers to lists of individuals and/or organizations.

Direct mail package: A mailing consisting of multiple enclosures inserted into an outer envelope, all of which promote the same or related products. The minimum contents for a direct mail package include a letter, order card, and brochure.

Directory compiled lists: Lists gathered from education directories published annually by each state.

District-level purchase: A purchase where the decision to buy was made at the district level without input from building level personnel.

Dunning: Usually a series of collection letters accompanying bills. These letters usually use language that increasingly urges customers to pay their bills as the series progresses.

Format: The physical characteristics of direct mail promotions. Major categories include catalog, direct mail package, self-mailer, and co-op deck.

Front-end response: The total response or number of orders received from a mailing.

Fund-raising: Any activity that yields school funds outside the normal school budget.

Gross contribution per thousand: The difference between the total sales revenue from a given promotion and the cost of goods associated with servicing that revenue divided by the number of thousand pieces of promotion distributed. The amount after cost of goods is expenses left to pay for promotion, overhead, and profit. If a promotion of 10,000 pieces results in $5,000 in sales, and the cost of goods to service those sales is $2,000, then the gross contribution per thousand is $300.

Guarantee:	An assurance of the quality or the length of use to be expected from a product offered for sale. Often includes a promise of reimbursement.
High ticket:	Expensive. Generally over a $500 selling price in the school market.
Inserting:	The process of physically placing the components of a mailing into the outer mailer.
Lead:	A prospect who has expressed an interest in further information about a product or service.
Lead getting:	The process of generating requests for additional information about a product or service.
Low ticket:	Inexpensive. Generally under a $500 selling price in the school market.
Media:	A means of communication that reaches or influences people widely such as radio, television, newspapers, and magazines.
Net contribution per thousand:	The difference between the total sales revenue from a given promotion and the sum of the cost of goods, promotion expense, and overhead associated with servicing that revenue divided by the number of thousand pieces of promotion distributed.

Net contribution per thousand (continued):	If a promotion of 10,000 pieces results in $10,000 in sales, the cost of goods to service those sales is $2,000, the promotion expense is $3,000, and the overhead is 20% of sales, the net contribution per thousand is $300.
Odd-even zip split:	A common practice to enhance tracking results of offer and promotion format tests. The mailing lists are divided into two equal groups, one with addresses ending in odd number zip codes and the other with addresses ending in even number zip codes. The test is mailed to one group while the control or bulk is mailed to the other.
	If one is testing a premium offer vs no premium, the premium offer is mailed to the odd zips and the no premium offer is mailed to the even zip. Once the campaign is over, sales are tallied by odd vs even zip codes to analyze the results.
Offer:	The specific terms and conditions of a given solicitation. The major components of an offer include the price, premium, payment terms, guarantee, and expiration date.
Order device:	The vehicle used to respond to a promotion.
Orders per thousand:	The total number of orders received from a given promotion divided by the number of thousand pieces distributed. A mailing of

10,000 pieces that generates 100 orders is said to yield 10 orders per thousand.

Per pupil expenditure: The amount of money spent on instructional materials by an institution for each pupil enrolled.

Percent response: The total number of orders received divided by the total number of promotion pieces distributed. A mailing of 10,000 pieces that generates 100 orders is said to have yielded a 1% response.

Premium: An item offered free of charge.

Preview: The process of ordering a sample product for the express purpose of reviewing its content in order to make a purchasing decision. This process is most common in the purchasing of audio visual materials.

Promotion cost per thousand: The total cost of a promotion divided by the number of thousand pieces distributed. A mailing of 100 thousand pieces that cost $50,000 to create, print, bind, and distribute is said to have a promotion cost of $500 per thousand.

Purchase order phenomena: The practice by which schools place the majority of their orders on school purchase orders. This results in very few original order devices being returned to school marketers, thus making the tracking of response difficult.

Returns:	The number of units or dollar value of product returned by customers after shipment, usually for reasons of dissatisfaction or damage.
Revenue per thousand:	The total sales revenue from a given promotion divided by the number of thousand pieces of promotion distributed. A promotion of 10,000 pieces that results in $5,000 in sales is said to yield revenue of $500 per thousand.
Roll out:	The incorporation of a successful test concept into the bulk of a promotion campaign.
Scanning:	The process of perusing a promotion piece or advertisement in an attempt to determine if a more detailed reading of the material is warranted.
Segments:	Subsets of a market, usually based upon some demographic characteristic. For example, the school market may be divided into segments based upon small, medium, and large school enrollment size.
Self-mailer:	Any single promotion piece that mails by itself without an envelope. Selfmailers can vary greatly in size and shape and can be one dimensional or include pop-ups.

Space ad: A printed advertisement other than a classified ad which usually appears in a periodical such as a magazine.

Supplementary classroom materials: Any materials used in a classroom to enhance or expand upon the primary source of instruction.

Teaser copy: Copy employed in an ad or promotion piece to intrigue or entice the reader to investigate further.

Universe: All of the eligible members of any given market. The universe of elementary schools includes buildings that service grades K-3, 4-6, 5-8, K-6, K-8 and K-12.

Zip string: Any group of mailing labels sequenced in zip code order.

INDEX